NIGEL DAVIES

W9-BFP-025

THE
RULES
OF
WINNING
CHESS

EVERYMAN CHESS

Gloucester Publishers plc www.everymanchess.com

First published in 2009 by Gloucester Publishers plc (formerly Everyman Publishers plc), Northburgh House, 10 Northburgh Street, London EC1V 0AT

British Library Cataloguing-in-Publication Data
A catalogue record for this book is available from the British Library.

ISBN: 978 1 85744 596 1

Distributed in North America by The Globe Pequot Press, P.O Box 480, 246 Goose Lane, Guilford, CT 06437-0480.

All other sales enquiries should be directed to Everyman Chess, Northburgh House, 10 Northburgh Street, London EC1V 0AT
tel: 020 7253 7887 fax: 020 7490 3708
email: info@everymanchess.com; website: www.everymanchess.com

Everyman is the registered trade mark of Random House Inc. and is used in this work under licence from Random House Inc.

EVERYMAN CHESS SERIES
Chief advisor: Byron Jacobs
Commissioning editor: John Emms
Assistant editor: Richard Palliser

Typeset and edited by First Rank Publishing, Brighton.
Cover design by Horatio Monteverde.
Printed and bound in the US by Versa Press.

Contents

Bibliography

Books

500 Master Games by Savielly Tartakower and Dumont (Dover, 1975)

A Breviary of Chess by Savielly Tartakower (Butler & Tanner, 1937)

Descartes Error by Antonio Damasio (Vintage Books, 1994)

Dynamic Chess Strategy by Mihai Suba (Pergamon, 1991)

Education of a Speculator by Victor Niederhoffer (John Wiley & Sons, Inc, 1997)

Endgame Strategy by Mikhail Shereshevsky (Pergamon, 1985)

Grandmaster of Chess: The Complete Games of Paul Keres by Paul Keres (ARCO, 1977)

How to Open a Chess Game by Larry Evans, Vlastimil Hort, Bent Larsen, Tigran Petrosian and Lajos Portisch (RHM Press, 1974)

How to Play Chess Endings by Eugene Znosko-Borovsky (Dover, 1974)

Lasker's Manual of Chess by Emanuel Lasker (Printing-Craft Limited, 1932)

Mastery by George Leonard (Plume, 1992)

My Best Games of Chess, 1931-1954 by Savielly Tartakower (Hardinge Simpole, 2003)

My System by Aron Nimzowitsch (Quality Chess, 2007)

Shape Shifter by Geoff Thompson (Summersdale Publishers, 2005)

Striking Thoughts: Bruce Lee's Wisdom for Daily Living by John Little (Tuttle Publishing, 2000)

The Art of Peace by Morihei Ueshiba (Shambhala, 2005)

The Art of the Middle Game by Paul Keres and Alexander Kotov (Penguin, 1964)

The Book of Five Rings by Myamoto Musashi (Allison and Busby Limited, 1982)

The Morals of Chess by Benjamin Franklin (Tri-Arts Press, 1932)

The Unfettered Mind: Writings from a Zen Master to a Master Swordsman by Takuan Soho and William Scott Wilson (Kodansha America, Inc, 1988)

The Zen Way to the Martial Arts by Taisen Deshimura (Penguin Compass, 1982)
Think Like a Grandmaster by Alexander Kotov (Batsford, 1971)
Zen in the Martial Arts by Joe Hyams (Bantam Books, 1979)
ZOOM 001 by Stephan Zeuthen and Bent Larsen (Dansk Skakforlag, 1979)

Databases
Mega Database 2009
Chess Informants 1-73

Computer Chess Engines
Fritz 11

Introduction

Writing this book presented me with a challenge; the more that someone understands about chess the less important rules seem to be. Then I realized this is only because our ideas about chess become so deeply ingrained that we no longer need to voice them. They are still there but dwell in the subconscious mind.

So this project presented me with a unique opportunity: to give form to the many beliefs I have built up through some 40 years of playing and studying chess about how a chess game should be conducted. It also presented the challenge of stating them in a clear and concise way.

The list of rules that has emerged is a rather personal one and I am sure that many other players will disagree with both my views and priorities. I can only say that a player's guidelines cannot be decided by committee. My hope is that the reader will find some points of interest that may ultimately become incorporated into his or her own chess persona. I offer my rules to inspire rather than instruct, to stimulate thought and disagreement rather than blind obedience.

I have divided my rules into five different categories: the player, preparation, the opening, the middlegame and the endgame. To some extent this division is artificial, not least because the boundaries between these areas are often blurred. I hope that it will at least lend clarity to my presentation.

The reader may also be surprised at some of my sources, in that many of them are not specifically concerned with chess. To a large extent this reflects the universal nature of the chess struggle in that rules which apply to the player, board and pieces are analogous to those in other spheres.

I would like to express my appreciation to the many people who have acted as my mentors and teachers over the years and the many who continue to do so in my pursuit of lifelong learning. Special mention should go to the former British

Veterans Champion Samuel Roberts, FIDE Master John Littlewood, Grandmaster and former Soviet Chess Champion Lev Psakhis, former World squash champion and speculator Victor Niederhoffer, Master Lam Kam-Chuen and Sifu Steven Williams. Most of all there is my son Sam whose curiosity about the world is a constant source of inspiration.

Nigel Davies
Southport
August 2009
http://www.tigerchess.com

Chapter One

The Player

"The Game of Chess is not merely an idle amusement, several very valuable qualities of the mind, useful in the course of human life, are to be acquired and strengthened by it, so as to become habits ready on all occasions for life is a kind of Chess, in which we have points to gain, and competition or adversaries to contend with, and in which there is a vast variety of good and ill events, that are, in some degree, the effect of prudence, or want of it. By playing at Chess then, we may learn:

First, Foresight...

Second, Circumspection...

Third, Caution...

And lastly, We learn by Chess the habit of not being discouraged by present bad appearances in the state of our affairs the habit of hoping for a favourable chance, and that of persevering in the secrets of resources."

Benjamin Franklin (*The Morals of Chess*)

The most important aspect of winning chess is the cultivation of certain personal qualities. Over time I've become increasingly aware of the importance of these traits having spent years rubbing shoulders with both winners and losers. Winners have certain things in common that I believe provide the bedrock of their success. And losers too have certain traits which lead them towards self sabotage.

Chess lore is not particularly rich in material about how to cultivate these traits, perhaps assuming that players either come to the game with them already intact or develop them through play. My own belief is that they may also be honed through other sources as they are in fields such as martial arts. For this reason I've drawn heavily on sources outside of chess for this section.

1) Train with deadly seriousness

"You must be deadly serious in training. When I say that, I do not mean that you should be reasonably diligent or moderately in earnest. I mean that your opponent must always be present in your mind, whether you sit or stand or walk or raise your arms."

Gichin Funakoshi

"Progress comes to those who train and train; reliance on secret techniques will get you nowhere."

Moreihei Ueshiba

"What I have discovered is that anyone with average ability and a strong desire can become a top amateur in any chosen field if they invest 3,000 hours into its study and practice. That amounts to one hour a day, six days a week for ten years. If the same 'average' person wanted to become a world beater they would need to invest 10,000 hours, which is the same weekly commitment extended over thirty years. Of course, if you were to increase your investment your return would be greater and the time to fruition proportionately shorter."

Geoff Thompson (*Shape-Shifter*)

There's no doubt in my mind that the number one prerequisite of success in any field is to immerse yourself in it, body and soul. Every strong chess player has had a period in their lives in which they ate, slept and breathed chess, but curiously enough such dedication has not carried with it the same degree of respectability as other fields. Accordingly many chess players appear to have downplayed the amount of time they've spent on the game, perhaps so that people will ascribe their feats to natural talent. But don't be deceived, this is simply not the case.

The figure of 10,000 hours is sometimes quoted as the time taken to achieve excellence in a particular field, and assuming a reasonable degree of talent for the game plus enough opportunity to play, this seems to be a reasonable ballpark figure to get the International Master title. Further progress beyond that may take incrementally greater effort, and indeed many players don't progress from being International Masters to Grandmasters.

Clearly there are going to be many ways that a simple count of man-hours should be qualified, for example the quality of someone's training efforts is going to be vital. But this nevertheless provides a vital insight into just what it takes to achieve a high level in chess.

In my own career I had been an International Master for 10 years before deciding to dedicate myself towards achieving the Grandmaster title. So from late 1992 I focussed my efforts exclusively on an increase in playing strength and a hunt for title norms. I set up a tournament schedule for 1993 and beyond, and between events lived in a caravan with nothing but chess books, a computer and a rigorous time-table. Fortunately I had secured the title by August 1993 so this Spartan existence did not have to last too long.

Here's one of my games from this period, against the Hungarian theoretician Peter Lukacs, which clearly showed the benefits of this level of dedication:

Game 1
N.Davies-P.Lukacs
Budapest 1993
Catalan Opening

---

1 d4

Already a sign of a different level of preparedness. Against a player with Lukacs' expertise in the openings I would normally have preferred some kind of flank opening.

1...d5 2 ♘f3 ♘f6 3 c4 e6 4 g3 dxc4 5 ♗g2 ♗d7 6 ♘e5 ♗c6 7 ♘xc6 ♘xc6 8 0-0 ♗e7

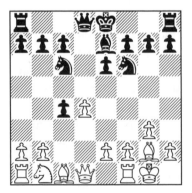

Strangely enough I had half ex-

pected this move, even though it had rarely been played at the time. During my studies I had noticed that Lukacs' compatriot Istvan Farago had played this move and guessed that it might crop up.

The alternatives seem quite good for White. For example:

a) 8...♘xd4?! is met by 9 ♗xb7 ♖b8 10 ♗g2 ♗c5 11 ♘d2 c3 12 bxc3 ♘b5 13 ♕c2 0-0 14 a4, as in B.Gulko-V.Korchnoi, Amsterdam 1989.

b) 8...♕d7 9 e3 ♖b8 10 ♕e2 b5 11 a4 a6 12 axb5 axb5 13 b3 cxb3 14 ♘d2 ♗e7 15 ♘xb3 0-0 16 ♗d2! ♖fc8 17 ♖fc1 ♘d5 was K.Georgiev-V.Anand, Wijk aan Zee 1989, and here 18 h4!, intending h4-h5-h6, would have kept an edge for White according to Anand.

9 e3 0-0

In a later game, S.Polgar-A.Maric, Tilburg 1994, Black tried to improve on this with 9...♕d7 but after 10 ♕a4 ♘b4 11 ♕xd7+ ♘xd7 12 ♘d2 ♘b6 13 ♗xb7 ♖b8 14 ♗f3 White was better thanks to the useful pair of bishops.

10 ♘d2 ♘a5 11 ♕a4 c6

On 11...c5 White's simplest would be 12 dxc5 ♗xc5 13 ♘xc4 ♘xc4 14

♕xc4, with an edge because of the powerful bishop on g2.

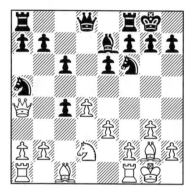

12 b4 c3 13 bxa5 cxd2 14 ♗xd2

White's strong bishop pair and action along the b- and c-files give him all the play here, notwithstanding the doubled a-pawns.

14...♘d5 15 ♖ab1 ♕d7 16 ♖fc1 ♖fc8 17 ♕b3 ♖ab8 18 a4 h6 19 h4 ♗d6 20 e4 ♘e7 21 ♕b2

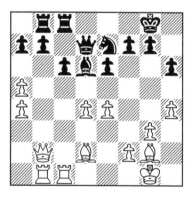

Torturing Black with the possibility of ♗d2-c3 followed by a later d4-d5. Accordingly he makes the following bid for freedom.

21...b5 22 axb6 ♖xb6

22...axb6 would have kept Black's

pawns intact but would have also left him with very little counterplay.

23 ♕a1 ♖xb1 24 ♖xb1 f5

This breaks up White's powerful pawn centre and gets access to the d5-square. But the downside is that it creates weaknesses along the e-file.

24...c5 would have been a better try, after which 25 ♗c3 cxd4 26 ♗xd4 f6 would have left Black worse but on the board.

25 ♖e1 ♖d8 26 ♕a2 ♔h8 27 h5 fxe4 28 ♖xe4 ♘d5 29 ♕c4 ♖f8 30 ♕e2 ♘c7 31 ♗h3 ♖f6 32 ♔g2

Trying to improve my position in leisurely style.

32...c5 33 ♗c3 ♖f8?!

It would have been more stubborn to play 33...♘d5, though this is still good for White after 34 ♗b2 c4 35 ♕xc4 ♕b7 36 ♕c2.

34 ♗xe6 ♕c6

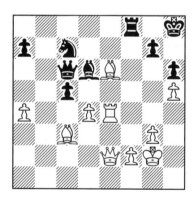

35 ♔g1?!

Missing a stronger option in 35 ♕g4! threatening 36 d5 or even 36 ♕xg7+ followed by 37 d5+. This variation would have been immediately decisive.

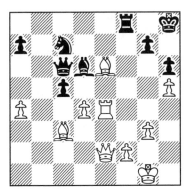

35...c4?!

Black could have defended more stubbornly with 35...♘d5 when I would have had to find the variation 36 ♗xd5 ♕xd5 37 dxc5 ♗xc5 38 ♕g4 ♗xf2+ 39 ♔h2 ♕b7 40 ♕g6 ♔g8 41 ♗b4! threatening both 42 ♗xf8 and 42 ♖e7.

36 ♗xc4 ♕xa4 37 d5

Unveiling the dark-squared bishop on c3 sets up a new target: Black's king. **37...♕d7 38 ♕e3 ♔g8 39 ♕e2 a6 40 ♖g4 ♖f7 41 ♕e4 ♘b5 42 ♗b2 ♕a7 43 ♕e8+ ♗f8 44 d6! ♕xf2+ 45 ♔h1 1-0**

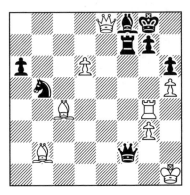

After 45...♕f3+ 46 ♔h2 ♕f2+ 47 ♔h3 Black's checks have run out.

2) Educate yourself

"Despite my many years of martial arts study, I recognize how little I really know compared with true masters of the arts. Only by constantly exposing myself to someone better than I have I been able to improve. It is inspiring to know that even the masters have masters and that we are all learners."

Joe Hyams (*Zen in the Martial Arts*)

"It is not how much you have learned, but how much you have absorbed in what you have learned – the best techniques are the simple ones executed right."

Bruce Lee

"The boy doesn't have a clue about chess, and there's no future at all for him in this profession."

Mikhail Botvinnik on Anatoly Karpov

It's important to note that a good chess education is mainly about educating oneself. In the heat of battle it is simply not enough to rely on second hand ideas about what you think you are supposed to do. Your thoughts must be your own thoughts, which means thoroughly internalizing any ideas you come across even if the original spark came from a coach or mentor. A chess player must be self educated to have any hope of long-term success.

For this reason the best teachers inspire rather than drill. A player's job is to seek out such sources of insight, whether they be mentors, good books or even just hanging out with good players. Any insights gained should then be followed up diligently until they become part of the player's being.

Like with many players, my own chess education might appear somewhat haphazard. Although I have never had a formal one-to-one chess lesson I've found sources of inspiration everywhere. In my early teens a local strong player who once won the British Veterans Championship, Sam Roberts, used to invite me to his home just about every Sunday and we played game after game. I was also inspired by the strongest local player, John Littlewood; every game I got to play against him was like attending a master class.

Many players complain about lacking a good teacher yet most of the great players from history have written books. I read both *Lasker's Manual of Chess* and Capablanca's *Chess Fundamentals* several times and then worked my way through the game collections of every World Champion plus those of great players who did not quite make it. Unlike many subjects, you can learn a lot about chess by reading the right books.

The influence of these mentors is largely invisible, though John Littlewood and later Leonid Stein did have an influence over my opening repertoire which shows through to this day. One of the more obvious things I picked up on was Littlewood's treatment of the Philidor Defence with 1 e4 e5 2 ♘f3 d6 3 d4 exd4 4 ♘xd4 g6, an idea that originally stemmed from Bent Larsen but which Littlewood made his own. This baton of knowledge was passed down to me and can clearly be shown in Godena-Davies (see Game 3).

Game 2
D.Sherman-J.Littlewood
Lloyds Bank Masters,
London 1973
Philidor Defence

1 e4 e5 2 ♘f3 d6 3 d4 exd4 4 ♘xd4 g6

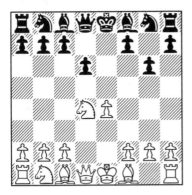

Although it was originally adopted by Bent Larsen, this should really be known as the Larsen-Littlewood Variation given John's extensive usage.

5 ♘c3 ♝g7 6 ♝c4

Although this looks like an active move, the bishop is not that well placed on this square.

White's best is probably to play ♝e3, ♕d2 and castle long, and indeed this has become the main line.

6...♘c6 7 ♘xc6 bxc6 8 0-0 ♜b8!?

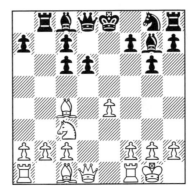

Delaying the development of the kingside to set up immediate b-file pressure. Black's next move also breaks 'the rules' by developing the queen early, but once again White must deal with some direct threats.

9 f4 ♕h4!? 10 ♕d3

In a later game, D.Pritchard-J.Littlewood, Morecambe 1975, White played 10 ♕e1 after which 10...♕h5!? (the exchange of queens would leave Black no worse) 11 ♝e3 ♘h6 12 ♝b3 0-0 13 ♝xa7 ♜b4 led to double-edged play.

10...♘h6!?

Yet another original move. By going to h6 Black takes all the sting out of e4-e5, keeps the h8-a1 diagonal open for the bishop on g7 and maintains the possibility of ...f7-f5.

11 h3 0-0 12 b3?

As we shall soon see this is a tactical mistake. Littlewood is now in his element: tactics and combinations.

12...d5! 13 exd5 cxd5 14 ♗xd5 ♗f5 15 ♕f3 c6 16 ♗xc6

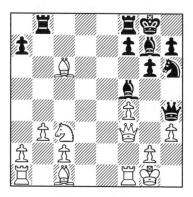

16...♗g4! 17 hxg4

Black wins a piece after 17 ♕f2 ♕xf2+ 18 ♔xf2 ♗xc3, whilst 17 ♕e3 can be powerfully met by 17...♖fd8 threatening 18...♗d4.

17...♗d4+ 18 ♗e3 ♘xg4 19 ♕xg4

Or 19 ♖fe1 ♕h2+ 20 ♔f1 ♘xe3+ 21 ♖xe3 ♕h1+ 22 ♔e2 ♕xa1 etc.

19...♗xe3+ 0-1

Game 3
M.Godena-N.Davies
1st Saturday, Budapest 1993
Modern Defence

---

1 e4 g6 2 d4 ♗g7 3 ♘c3 d6 4 ♘ge2 ♘c6

This development of the queen's knight was one of the hallmarks of my handling of the Modern Defence. Black intends to follow up with ...e7-e5.

5 ♗e3 ♘f6 6 h3 e5 7 dxe5 ♘xe5

Arriving at a position very much akin to John Littlewood's pet Philidor line.

8 ♘g3 0-0

A safer option would have been 8...♗e6 9 ♕d2 ♘c4, but as I had to win this game I was prepared to play for complications.

9 ♕d2 ♖e8 10 0-0-0 b5!?

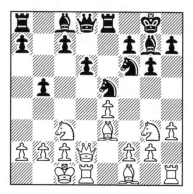

Sacrificing a pawn to open the b-file, which is probably not such a bad idea with opposite-side castling. There's a good chapter on this in *The Art of the Middle Game* by Paul Keres and Alexander Kotov. Many wonderful hours of chess lessons by two of the great players from history.

11 ♗xb5 ♗d7 12 ♗e2

My opponent did not like the look of 12 f4 because of 12...♗xb5 13 fxe5 ♖xe5 14 ♗d4 ♕e7, which gives Black compensation for the sacrificed exchange.

12...♕b8 13 f4 ♘c6 14 ♗f3 ♕b4

This followed by putting a rook on b8 will provoke a weakening of White's queenside.

15 a3 ♕b7 16 e5 ♖ab8

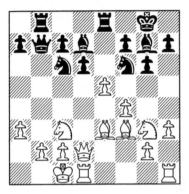

17 b3

After 17 ♘a4 Black can play 17...dxe5 18 fxe5 ♕b5: for example, 19 exf6 ♗xf6 20 b3 ♖xe3 21 ♕xd7 ♗g5 22 ♔b1 ♖xb3+ etc.

17...dxe5 18 fxe5 ♖xe5 19 ♘ge4 ♕a6

Correctly avoiding a preliminary exchange of knights on e4. After 19...♘xe4 20 ♘xe4 ♕a6 White can play 21 a4 when his defences continue to hold.

20 a4?

The losing move. White should have taken on f6 before Black gained the possibility of recapturing with his queen.

20...♘a5! 21 ♘xf6+ ♕xf6!

After this the veiled threats along the h8-a1 diagonal prove decisive. Perhaps White had set too much store on his next move; if so he is about to be

severely disappointed.

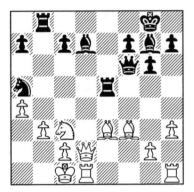

22 ♗d4 ♕d6!

The point of Black's play. Now after the capture of the rook on e5, Black can play ...♕a3+ followed by ...♘xb3.

23 ♘b1 ♖xb3!

Blasting away the last remnants of White's castled position.

24 ♗a1 ♕b6 0-1

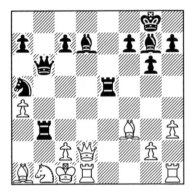

Black is threatening 25...♖xb1+, and the rook cannot be taken because White would lose his queen. Furthermore, after 25 ♘c3 both 25...♘c4 and 25...♖a3 would win for Black.

3) Be vigilant

*"You know the story of the three cats: there was a samurai who had a rat in his house
and could not get rid of it. He acquired a superb cat, stalwart and robust. But the rat was
quicker and simply made a fool of it. Then the samurai got another cat, more cunning and
astute. But the rat was on his guard and hid except when the cat was asleep. Then a Zen
monk from a nearby temple lent the samurai his own cat, the most ordinary-looking cat
you could imagine, that spent all its time drowsing and napping and paid no attention to
anything around it. The samurai shrugged and said the cat was no good, but the monk
insisted he keep it. So the cat stayed and slept and slept, and soon the rat grew bold again
and began trotting back and forth right in front of the cat, which showed absolutely no
interest in it. Then one day, with one swipe of its paw, it caught the rat and pinned it
down. Strength of body and technical skill are nothing, without vigilance of mind!"*

Taisen Deshimura (*The Zen Way to the Martial Arts*)

Vigilance is a hugely important aspect of chess, but one that's often underestimated. Just like the rat in the story above, players can be on their guard against a dangerous adversary. Yet when they play against someone they expect to beat they can become careless.

A similar phenomenon occurs when players have good positions: expecting to win they can easily lower their attention level and start to make mistakes. A similar loss of vigilance occurs when players are distracted during a game or think so deeply that they forget to look for what's under their noses.

How should someone increase their vigilance? Experience can play a part in that negative experiences can make someone try harder the next time. But perhaps the best method is through meditation, an age old technique used by Japanese swordsman.

Let's now take a look at a couple of examples of the need for vigilance. Grandmaster and former US Champion Frank James Marshall was one of the most naturally vigilant players to have graced the chequered board and he evidently considered this an important quality by stating: "In chess, attention is more important than concentration." Indeed he used his superior powers of vigilance to become one of the greatest players in history.

In the following game he uses his vigilance against the deep Akiba Rubinstein. Rubinstein outplays Marshall, but it is the latter's vigilance that carries the day. With one false move Rubinstein is defeated, just as in the tale of the three cats.

Game 4
A.Rubinstein-F.Marshall
Lodz 1908
Semi-Slav Defence

1 d4 d5 2 ♘f3 ♘d7 3 c4 e6 4 ♘c3 c6 5 e4 dxe4 6 ♘xe4 ♘gf6 7 ♗d3 ♘xe4 8 ♗xe4 ♘f6 9 ♗c2 ♗b4+ 10 ♗d2 ♕a5 11 0-0 ♗xd2 12 ♘xd2 0-0

Black's opening has been rather passive and with his next move White cements his space advantage.

13 c5! b6 14 ♘b3 ♕b4 15 ♕f3 ♗a6 16 ♖fd1 bxc5 17 dxc5

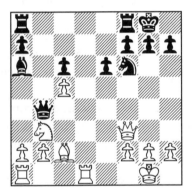

17...♖fd8?!

Marshall characteristically goes for active counterplay. 17...♘d5 is the more solid choice but he was probably concerned about 18 ♖d4 followed by ♕f3-h5, when White has his queen, rook and bishop in the vicinity of Black's king.

18 ♕xc6 ♗b7 19 ♕c7 ♘d5 20 ♕e5 ♘f4 21 ♖xd8+ ♖xd8 22 ♖d1

22 ♕c7 was a more convincing way to play it, as after 22...♖f8 23 c6 ♗a8

Black's bishop on a8 is shut out of the game.

Perhaps Rubinstein had seen the possibility of transposing into an endgame, which was his happy hunting ground. But the apparent neutralization of Black's counterplay appears to have lowered his vigilance.

22...♖xd1+ 23 ♗xd1 f6 24 a3! fxe5 25 axb4 ♗xg2 26 f3

This looks as if it safeguards White's king by giving it the f2-square, which might well have been another nail in White's psychological coffin.

26 b5 was a better way to play it, with good winning chances for White.

26...e4! 27 c6? exf3

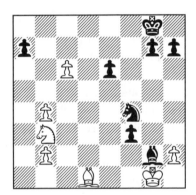

28 c7??

A disastrous oversight.

28 ♔f2 was mandatory, though Black would then be able to draw with 28...♘d5.

28...♘h3 mate (0-1)

The next game is a more recent encounter between another two great players, Bent Larsen and Paul Keres. After having enjoyed a slight edge throughout and having a position that it seems cannot be lost, Larsen relaxes his vigilance for just a couple of moves. And after 61...♕g3! he suddenly finds himself totally lost.

Game 5
B.Larsen-P.Keres
San Antonio 1972
English Opening

---

1 c4 e6 2 ♘c3 c5 3 ♘f3 ♘f6 4 g3 ♘c6 5 ♗g2 ♗e7 6 d4 d5 7 cxd5 ♘xd5 8 ♘xd5 exd5 9 dxc5 ♗xc5 10 a3

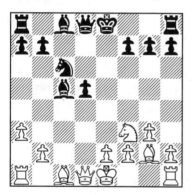

10...♗f5

According to Keres, he should have stopped White's next move with 10...a5!.

11 b4 ♗b6 12 ♗b2 0-0 13 ♘d4! ♗xd4

And here 13...♘xd4 14 ♗xd4 ♗e4 would have been fine for Black.

14 ♗xd4 ♖e8 15 ♖a2 ♕d7

15...♗e4! was the right idea here too. Now White starts to get slightly the better of it.

16 0-0 ♗h3 17 ♖d2 ♗xg2 18 ♔xg2 a5 19 ♗c5 axb4 20 axb4 ♖e5 21 e3 ♖d8 22

b5 ♘e7 23 ♗xe7 ♕xe7 24 ♕b3 h5 25 ♖d4 ♖d6 26 ♖fd1 ♕e8 27 h4

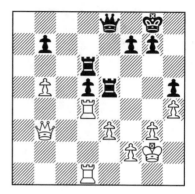

27...♖b6?!

27...g6 was stronger.

28 ♖xd5 ♖xb5 29 ♖xe5! ♖xe5 30 ♕xb7 ♖c5 31 ♖d6 g6 32 ♖d7 ♕e6 33 ♖d8+ ♔g7 34 ♕b4 ♕c4 35 ♕b2+ ♕c3 36 ♕b7 ♖f5 37 ♕e7 ♕b2 38 ♕f8+ ♔h7 39 ♕g8+ ♔h6 40 ♖d2 ♕g7 41 ♕a8 ♔h7

The immediate 41...♕c3! was a better idea.

42 e4 ♕c3!

The only move. After 42...♖e5 White has a strong reply in 43 ♖d7!.

43 exf5 ♕xd2 44 ♕b7 ♔g8 45 f6

White could maintain a nagging edge with 45 fxg6 fxg6 46 ♕e4, but he gets tempted by the possibility of putting a pawn on f6.

45...♕d8 46 ♕c6 ♔h7 47 ♕c3 ♕d5+ 48 f3 ♕a2+ 49 ♔h3 ♕b1 50 ♔g2 ♕a2+ 51 ♔f1 ♕a6+! 52 ♔e1 ♕e6+ 53 ♔f2 ♕a2+ 54 ♔g1 ♕b1+ 55 ♔g2 ♕a2+ 56 ♔h3 ♕b1 57 g4 ♕h1+ 58 ♔g3 ♕g1+

White has been better the whole game but should now accede to a draw by perpetual check. Instead he continues playing for a win in what looks like an 'unloseable' position and falls into one of the nastiest snares I've ever seen.

59 ♔f4? ♕h2+ 60 ♔g5??

It wasn't too late to avoid the cliff with 60 ♔e4, though Black would have all the chances after 60...♕xh4.

60...♕g3!

This move deserves another diagram. After having been complacently nursing a slight edge White suddenly finds himself totally lost. Black threatens 61...hxg4 and White's queen is tied down to defending against mate with ...♕e5. An object lesson in the need for vigilance!

61 ♕e3 hxg4 62 ♕f4 ♕xf3 63 ♕xg4 ♕e3+ 64 ♕f4 ♕e2! 65 ♕g3 ♕b5+ 66 ♔f4 ♕f5+ 67 ♔e3 ♕xf6

So Black goes a pawn up with a win in sight. Larsen must have been totally demoralized by this sudden turn of events.

68 ♕g5 ♕f1 69 ♕g4 ♕e1+ 70 ♔d3 ♕e6 71 ♕f4 ♔g7 72 ♕d4+ f6 73 ♕b4 ♕f5+ 74 ♔e2 ♔h6 75 ♔e1 ♔h5 76 ♕c4 ♕g4 77 ♕c5+ ♔xh4 78 ♕e7 ♕f5 79 ♕b4+ ♔h5 80 ♕c4 g5 81 ♕f7+ ♔h4 82 ♕f8 ♔g3 83 ♕a3+ ♔f3 84 ♕d6+ ♔g2 85 ♕d2+ ♔h3 86 ♕d7+ f5 87 ♕g7 g4 88 ♕h8+ ♔g3 89 ♕e5+ f4 90 ♕b8 ♕c3+ 91 ♔d1 ♔g2 0-1

4) Flatten your heart

To *flatten your heart* is a saying from Chan Buddhism. There are equivalent sentiments in other cultures but none which seem quite as good to me. There's also the Samurai maxim: "The angry man will defeat himself in battle as in life." But this only deals with one emotional state, that of anger. *Flattening the heart* is more all encompassing, meaning that feelings such as an excess of joy should also be avoided lest this in turn weakens vigilance for the next battle.

When someone *flattens their heart* it does not mean they should become like a robot, without any emotions. It is more a case of not being distracted by the highs or lows that life throws at them. As soon as they allow their mood to become dependent on external events, which lie beyond their control, they will be giving up their mastery of life and find themselves buffeted around wildly.

A good example is when someone gets upset by something that's said to them and spends the entire day brooding over it. Essentially they are losing a day. They may believe that their day has been ruined, but essentially they are ruining it themselves by the way they react.

One magnificent example of this being applied to the chessboard was Savielly Tartakower's victory in the Hastings tournament of 1945/46. Here is what Tartakower himself wrote about it:

"My success was explained by some well-wishing chroniclers from the psychological point of view as due to my will to win; whilst from the technical point of view emphasis was laid on my creative and imaginative treatment of the endings which procured for me many an additional half point (against Denker, Prins, Sir George Thomas and E. G. Sergeant).

"Nevertheless, in my opinion the true cause of my triumph resided in the moral basis I had imposed on myself throughout the contest. As I had rightly supposed, the effects, or, at any rate, the depressing recollection of the great miseries, losses and anguish that were suffered during the war with Hitler still weighed heavily on the spirits of all the participants, even including those coming from the neutral countries (Sweden, Switzerland) or from fortunate America.

"Consequently, I resolved to concentrate all my efforts on not thinking about it at all; that is to say, on banishing it from my memory for the duration of the tournament, all these phantoms of the recent past: and this ensured my tranquillity of spirit and serenity of mind, both attributes so vitally necessary for any victory in the realm of sport."

Here is one of Tartakower's Hastings games, a crushing win over Herman Steiner:

Game 6
H.Steiner-S.Tartakower
Hastings 1945/46
French Defence

1 e4 e6 2 d4 d5 3 ♘c3 ♘f6 4 ♗g5 ♗e7 5 e5 ♘e4

Tartakower's patented line. Although its reputation is somewhat shaky, the Armenian Grandmaster Smbat Lputian tried to rehabilitate it a few years ago.

6 ♗xe7 ♕xe7 7 ♘xe4 dxe4

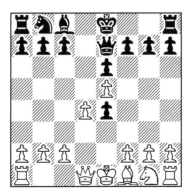

8 c3

V.Tseshkovsky-S.Lputian, Kropotkin 1995, went 8 ♕e2 b6 9 0-0-0 ♗b7 10 g3! c5 11 ♗g2 ♘c6 12 dxc5 0-0 13 ♗xe4 ♘xe5 14 f4 ♗xe4 15 ♕xe4 ♘g4 16 ♕f3, but even this isn't so clear after 16...f5!? (rather than Lputian's 16...♘f6), when Black secures e4 for his knight. Tartakower, by the way, recommended 10...♘d7 followed by 11...f5 against this line.

8...0-0 9 ♕c2

Black is doing well after both 9 ♕g4

f5 10 exf6 ♕xf6 (J.Capablanca-S.Tartakower, Budapest 1929) and 9 ♕e2 c5 10 f3 f6! (Golmayo-S.Tartakower, Barcelona 1929).

9...f5 10 0-0-0

After 10 exf6 ♕xf6 Black gets excellent counterplay.

10...c5 11 f3 cxd4 12 cxd4

12 ♖xd4 ♘c6 13 ♖d1 ♘xe5 14 fxe4 ♘g4 would also have been very unpleasant for White.

12...♗d7! 13 ♔b1 ♖c8 14 ♕b3 ♘c6 15 fxe4 fxe4

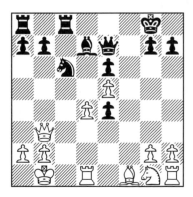

16 ♕e3?!

It's far too risky to take the e4-pawn. 16 ♘e2 instead would have been wiser.

16...♘b4 17 ♘e2

And not 17 ♕xe4? because of 17...♗a4 18 b3 ♗e8, whilst 17 a3 is refuted by 17...♗a4 18 b3 ♘d5.

17...♗a4! 18 b3

Forced: if 18 ♖c1 there would follow 18...♗c2+ 19 ♔a1 ♘d3 20 ♖xc2 ♖xc2 21 ♕xe4 ♕b4 etc.

18...♘d5 19 ♕h3

White would lose immediately after 19 ♕xe4 because of 19...♗xb3 20 axb3

♕a3 21 ♕d3 ♘c3+ 22 ♘xc3 ♕xb3+ 23 ♔a1 ♖xc3 24 ♕b1 ♕a4+ etc.

19...♗d7 20 ♔b2 a5 21 ♖c1

After 21 a3 Tartakower intended 21...a4 22 b4 ♘xb4 23 axb4 ♕xb4+ 24 ♔a1 a3 25 ♖b1 ♕d2 26 ♕b3 ♖c2 and White is defenceless against the threat of 26...a2.

21...♕g5!

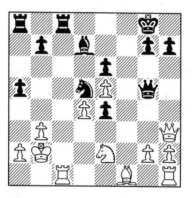

The key move, penetrating White's

defences via the d2-square.

22 ♖c4

If 22 ♖d1 Black can play 22...♘e3 23 ♖e1 ♘g4 threatening both 24...♘f2 and 24...♕d2+.

22...♕d2+ 23 ♔b1 ♖xc4 24 bxc4 ♘e3 25 g4 ♕d1+ 26 ♔b2 ♘xc4+ 27 ♔c3 ♕d2+ 0-1

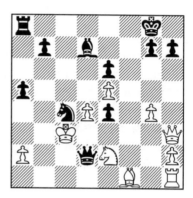

White is mated after 28 ♔b3 ♕b2+ 29 ♔xc4 ♕b4 mate.

5) Be your own sternest critic

"Failure is the key to success; each mistake teaches us something."

Moreihei Ueshiba

One of the most important qualities a chess player can cultivate is to effectively learn from his losses. To do so requires several abilities, not least of which is enough humility to admit that one has made a mistake in the first place. Those who make excuses for their defeats will never even look for the true cause. This in turn will make it hard for them to eliminate any weaknesses in their game.

Once weaknesses have been correctly identified it then requires willpower to do something about it. A classic example is that of Alexander Alekhine who lost his World Championship title to Max Euwe in 1935. For the return match Alekhine repaired his health by giving up alcohol and went on to win a crushing victory. Here's a game from this second match.

Game 7
A.Alekhine-M.Euwe
World Championship
(24th game), Holland 1937
Semi-Tarrasch Defence

1 ♘f3 d5 2 c4 e6 3 d4 ♘f6 4 ♘c3 c5 5 cxd5 ♘xd5 6 g3 cxd4 7 ♘xd5 ♕xd5 8 ♕xd4

Going into the endgame is a very disciplined decision; White is prepared to grind out a small edge. Two years earlier Alekhine's play was characterized by impatience more than anything.

8...♕xd4 9 ♘xd4 ♗b4+ 10 ♗d2 ♗xd2+ 11 ♔xd2

White is slightly better here because his kingside fianchetto will make it

difficult for Black to develop his queenside. But will it really be enough for a win?

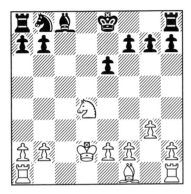

11...♔e7 12 ♗g2 ♖d8 13 ♔e3 ♘a6?!

The knight is not good on this square.

After 13...e5 White can keep a little something with 14 ♘b5 ♘c6 15 ♘c7 ♖b8 16 ♘d5+, but this should be quite tenable for Black.

14 ♖ac1 ♖b8 15 a3 ♗d7 16 f4 f6 17 ♗e4!

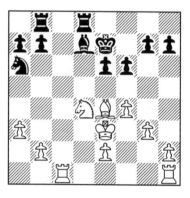

Cleverly trying to get more black pawns to go to light squares (17...f5) and make Black's remaining bishop bad.

17...♗e8

After 17...e5? 18 fxe5 fxe5 19 ♘f3 ♔f6 20 ♖hd1 Black would be defenceless against the threat of 21 ♖d6+.

18 b4

Threatening to win the knight with 19 b5.

18...♖d7 19 f5 ♘c7

This loses a pawn but 19...e5 20 ♘e6 would hardly be better.

20 fxe6 ♘xe6 21 ♘xe6 ♔xe6 22 ♗xh7 f5 23 ♖c5 g6 24 ♗g8+ ♔f6 25 ♖hc1 ♖e7+ 26 ♔f2

White is just a pawn up though the win requires good technique. Alekhine plays it in exemplary fashion.

26...♗c6 27 ♗d5 ♖be8 28 ♖e1 ♗xd5 29 ♖xd5 g5 30 ♖d6+ ♔e5?

After this Black finds his king in trouble. 30...♖e6 was better.

31 ♖ed1

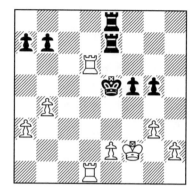

31...g4

If 31...♖e6 there follows 32 ♖d7 ♖8e7 33 ♖xe7 ♖xe7 34 h4, setting up a passed pawn.

32 ♖1d5+ ♔e4 33 ♖d4+ ♔e5 34 ♔e3 ♖e6 35 ♖4d5+ ♔f6+ 36 ♔f4 ♔g6 37 ♖xe6+ ♖xe6 38 ♖e5 ♖a6

Or 38...♖f6 39 e4 fxe4+ 40 ♔xg4 ♖f2 41 h4 and the two connected passed pawns will ensure victory.

39 ♖xf5 ♖xa3 40 ♖b5! b6 41 ♔xg4 1-0

Searching for weaknesses in your play as a whole can also be extended to the way you think during a game. The process by which someone searches for weaknesses in their ideas is known as falsification, an idea which stems from the father of the scientific method, Karl Popper. To Popper, testing a theory did not mean finding evidence to support it; instead it was a process of attempting to show it was false.

Most people tend not to do this, looking instead to confirm their ideas by finding supporting evidence. Yet strong chess players turn out to be excellent falsifiers, as research by Michelle Cowley and Ruth Byrne has shown. Here's the abstract to a paper they published in 2004.

"Falsification may demarcate science from non-science as the rational way to test the truth of hypotheses. But experimental evidence from studies of reasoning shows that people often find falsification difficult. We suggest that domain expertise may facilitate falsification. We consider new experimental data about chess experts' hypothesis testing. The results show that chess masters were readily able to falsify their plans. They generated move sequences that falsified their plans more readily than novice players, who tended to confirm their plans. The finding that experts in a domain are more likely to falsify their hypotheses has important implications for the debate about human rationality."

The fact that chess players should have this trait makes perfect sense; by being their own sternest critics they find out what's wrong with their ideas before their opponents do. Can this trait be acquired and developed? I believe so. For example, playing against stronger players the pain of defeat is only avoided by becoming a strong falsifier. Analysing your games with a stronger player will also help develop the falsification muscle, partly by having your thought processes 'corrected' and partly through picking up their habits via osmosis.

If there are no strong players available, either for playing games against or analysing with, there is an interesting alternative in correspondence chess. When both players have more time to think the quality of the play can increase dramatically, thus putting greater emphasis on the quality of a player's analysis rather than practical skills such as clock handling and alertness. The legendary Paul Keres played a large number of correspondence games in his youth and he developed into a formidable analyst and calculator. Needless to say, the benefits can only be felt if one does not rely on a computer to find the moves.

6) Don't think, feel

"Don't think – FEEL. Feeling exists here and now when not interrupted and dissected by ideas or concepts. The moment we stop analyzing and let go, we can start really seeing, feeling – as one whole."

Bruce Lee

"A great many people have mastered the multiplication tables of chess nowadays and even know its logarithm tables by heart. Therefore an attempt should occasionally be made to prove that two times two can also make five."

Mikhail Tal

Chess is often portrayed as a game of logic and reason yet in reality it is highly intuitive. It is beyond the capabilities of even the fastest computer to calculate out every possible line of play. Thus we have to 'guess', or rather intuit the value of different moves and their consequences. And for the best players this goes way beyond knowing what they should do when a particular pattern arises.

Intuition is in evidence when a player sacrifices material for some other factors such as time and space, such 'irregular' patterns calling for mental abilities way beyond the usually drudge work of applied technique. Certain players are well known for such intuitive abilities, for example Mikhail Tal. In the following game we see a wonderful example of his extraordinary abilities.

> *Game 8*
> **M.Tal-B.Larsen**
> Candidates Semi-final
> (10th game), Bled 1965
> *Sicilian Defence*

1 e4 c5 2 ♘f3 ♘c6 3 d4 cxd4 4 ♘xd4 e6 5 ♘c3 d6 6 ♗e3 ♘f6 7 f4 ♗e7 8 ♕f3 0-0

This line eventually fell out of favour for White because of 8...e5, which was in fact played in J.Van der Wiel-B.Larsen, Lugano 1989.

After 9 ♘xc6 bxc6 10 f5 ♕a5 11 0-0-0 ♗b7 12 ♗c4 ♖d8 13 g4 d5 14 g5 dxc4 15

---

gxf6 ♗xf6 16 ♖xd8+ Black should have played 16...♗xd8 when his position would have been quite playable.

9 0-0-0 ♕c7

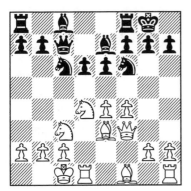

10 ♘db5

10 g4 is answered by 10...♘xd4 intending 11 ♖xd4 e5! 12 ♖c4 ♗xg4! etc.

10...♕b8 11 g4 a6 12 ♘d4 ♘xd4 13 ♗xd4 b5

13...e5 was right here too, though it would have been difficult to plunge into such a complicated line against Tal. After 14 g5 ♗g4! 15 ♕g2 exd4 16 ♖xd4 ♗e6 17 gxf6 ♗xf6 18 ♖d3 b5 the position would have been about equal.

14 g5 ♘d7 15 ♗d3 b4 16 ♘d5!

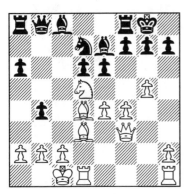

This remarkable move is one of Tal's most famous intuitive piece sacrifices. In return for the knight White gets a very dangerous attack on his opponent's king, but is it enough? When asked whether or not it was 'sound' Tal's comment was "I don't know, but I would play it again!"

16...exd5

The critical reply.

After 16...♖e8 White can play 17 e5!. For example, 17...exd5 18 e6 fxe6 (18...♘f8 19 ♗xh7+ ♘xh7 20 exf7+ ♔xf7 21 ♕h5+ gives White a winning attack) 19 ♕h5 ♘f8 20 ♗xh7+ ♘xh7 21 ♕xe8+ ♗f8 22 g6 ♗b7 23 ♕xe6+ ♔h8 24 ♕h3 followed by mate on h7.

17 exd5

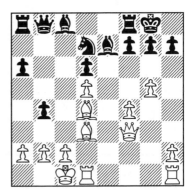

17...f5

Defending against the initial threat of 18 ♕e2, but perhaps this was not the best.

The critical line was 17...g6 when White has some tempting lines but nothing clear. After 18 ♖de1 (18 h4 can be answered by 18...♘c5: for example, 19 h5 ♘xd3+ 20 ♖xd3 ♗f5 21 hxg6 fxg6 22 ♖xh7 ♔xh7 23 ♖e3 ♕d8 24 ♕e2

♗xg5 25 fxg5 ♕xg5 wins) 18...♗d8 19 ♕h3 ♘e5 (19...♗b6 20 ♗xg6 wins on the spot: for example, 20...fxg6 21 ♖e7 etc) 20 ♕h6 ♗b6 21 ♗xe5 (21 fxe5 ♗xd4 22 ♖e4 ♗f2 23 ♖f1 ♕b6 24 e6 fxe6 defends everything) 21...dxe5 22 fxe5 ♗f2 (22...♗b7 23 ♖hf1 ♗xd5 24 ♖f4 ♖a7 25 ♖h4 f5 26 gxf6 threatens 27 ♗xg6) 23 ♖e2 ♕a7 24 ♖f1 ♗e3+ 25 ♔b1 ♗g4 and White's attack isn't quite getting through.

18 ♖de1 ♖f7

Fritz likes 18...♗d8 but then White can play 19 ♗xg7!? ♔xg7 20 ♕h5 ♖g8 21 ♗xf5 ♘f8 22 ♗d3 with a powerful attack for the sacrificed pieces. Computers have a tendency to misassess positions with material imbalance.

19 h4 ♗b7

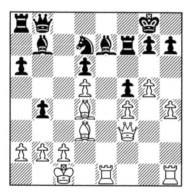

20 ♗xf5

20 h5 threatening 21 g6 also looks very strong.

20...♖xf5

After 20...♘f8 White can play 21 ♗xh7+ ♔xh7 (21...♘xh7 22 g6 ♖f8 23 ♕h5 wins on the spot) 22 h5 with the threat of 23 g6+.

21 ♖xe7 ♘e5!

The best try. After 21...♖f7 22 ♖xf7 ♔xf7 23 ♖e1 Black is defenceless against the infiltration of White's queen via g4, e4 or h5.

22 ♕e4 ♕f8

Finally getting his queen back to defend, but now White enjoys a material advantage plus an ongoing initiative.

23 fxe5 ♖f4 24 ♕e3

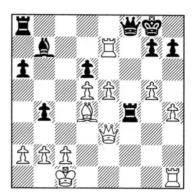

24...♖f3

The last chance was 24...♗xd5, though after 25 exd6 ♖xd4 26 ♕xd4 ♗xh1 27 b3 White's passed d-pawn outweighs Black's extra piece.

25 ♕e2 ♕xe7 26 ♕xf3 dxe5 27 ♖e1 ♖d8 28 ♖xe5 ♕d6 29 ♕f4 ♖f8 30 ♕e4 b3

After 30...♖f1+ 31 ♔d2 Black has no follow-up.

31 axb3 ♖f1+ 32 ♔d2 ♕b4+ 33 c3 ♕d6 34 ♗c5 ♕xc5 35 ♖e8+ ♖f8 36 ♕e6+ ♔h8 37 ♕f7 1-0

A magnificent game by Tal.

Can intuition be developed? Let's rephrase the question. Players are most intuitive when they are in the proverbial 'zone', so can someone engineer themselves into this zone? Chess players have traditionally tended to see being in the 'zone' as a gift from the gods but performers in other spheres have viewed it as something that can be arranged. Martial arts are again one of the more interesting models in which the practice of meditation is believed to help raise consciousness and develop an ability to act at a level beyond that of reason. I can understand why they'd want to do this, especially when playing with some very sharp swords. And once again this is an area that chess players might do well to explore.

There are some things I would not recommend. For example, there's the so-called *Blumenfeld rule* and variants thereof. The Blumenfeld rule in its original form involves writing your intended move down before playing it and then having a look round the board 'through the eyes of a patzer'. Besides the fact that writing your move down first has now been deemed to be illegal, my own experiments led to the conclusion that this rule tends to interrupt the flow of my thoughts, leading to a rather mechanical way of thinking.

Perhaps for some players a variation on Blumenfeld's rule can help reduce blunders; for example, to quietly whisper the move to yourself in long form (e.g. "bishop c2 takes f5") before doing the blunder check. But please bear in mind my deep reservations.

7) Learn patience

"If there is one thing that I have learned over the past forty-odd years on this beautiful planet it is that all things are possible, but they can take time to achieve. And the person that finds himself in too much of a hurry is destined for failure in one form or another. Impatience kills dreams."

Geoff Thompson (*Shape Shifter*)

Patience helps chess players on many different levels. First of all there's the patience required with trying to improve and continuing to work on your game even when it seems like you've reached a plateau. Plateaus are in fact quite normal as George Leonard describes in his best-selling book *Mastery*. And patience with the plateau is essential for continued growth:

"There's really no way around it. Learning any new skill involves relatively brief spurts of progress, each of which is followed by a slight decline to a plateau somewhat higher in most cases than that which preceded it. The curve above is necessarily idealized. In the actual learning experience, progress is less regular; the upward spurts vary; the plateaus have their own dips and rises along the way. But the general progression is almost always the same. To take the master's journey, you have to practice diligently, striving to hone your skills, to attain new levels of competence. But while doing so – and this is the inexorable fact of the journey – you also have to be willing to spend most of your time on a plateau, to keep practicing even when you seem to be getting nowhere."

The other way in which patience is invaluable is during an actual game; trying to rush things is a very common error. There are also situations in which it's very tempting to do so. For example, if your position is very good you might want to finish things off too quickly. And then there's the issue of playing against lower-rated players.

I've seen countless numbers of games lost by players who build up an advantage against a lower-rated player and then ruin everything in their impatient attempts to finish the game off quickly. They start to play for threats in the hope that their opponent will miss something and become increasingly frustrated when this does not happen. It's much better just to keep applying pressure when sooner or later there's a good chance that they'll crack. And the following effort by Tigran Petrosian is a case in point.

After a somewhat dubious opening Petrosian gradually outplays his opponent, patiently provoking weaknesses and improving the position of his pieces. White might well have held the game had he only needed to find a few good moves. But the wily Armenian's patient play made him find dozens of them, so it was no surprise when some mistakes finally appeared.

Game 9
J.Sefc-T.V.Petrosian
European Team
Championship, Vienna 1957
Sicilian Defence

1 e4 c5 2 ♘f3 e6 3 d4 cxd4 4 ♘xd4 ♘f6 5 ♘c3 d6 6 ♗e2 a6 7 ♗e3 b5

Playing this so early is somewhat risky and Petrosian soon finds himself in a difficult position.

8 ♗f3 e5 9 ♘f5 g6 10 ♘h6 ♗e6 11 ♘g4

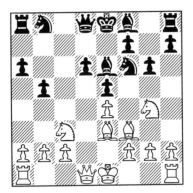

11...♘g8

A provocative-looking move to say the least. Black wants to keep his knight on the board because it can challenge for control of the d5-square. And meanwhile he reasons that the knight on g4 can simply be driven away.

12 ♘d5 ♘d7 13 ♗c1 ♗xd5 14 ♕xd5 h5 15 ♘e3 ♘gf6 16 ♕c6

16 ♕d1 would have been a bit better for White.

16...♕c8!

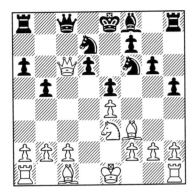

Petrosian shows characteristic patience, choosing to transpose into an endgame rather than worry about any drawish tendencies the position may contain. As we are about to discover, he is willing to keep the game going for a very long time.

17 ♕xc8+ ♖xc8 18 a4 b4 19 ♗e2 a5 20 f3 ♘b6 21 c4

21 ♗d2 might have been a better move, with the idea of playing 22 c3. After the text move White manages to block the position up but finds himself very passively placed.

21...♗h6

Rejecting the sharp 21...bxc3 22 bxc3 d5 because of the latent danger of the two bishops.

22 b3 ♘fd7 23 ♔f2 ♘c5 24 ♖b1 h4 25 ♖d1 ♖c6 26 ♗d3 ♗f4 27 h3

White probably believed that his

position was impregnable, and perhaps this is actually true. But there are lots of things Black can try, and this means considerable suffering for White.

27...♘bd7 28 ♗c2 ♘f8 29 ♗b2 ♘fe6 30 ♘d5 ♗g5 31 ♔f1 ♖f8 32 ♖e1 ♔d7 33 ♖bd1 ♔c8 34 ♔f2 ♔b7 35 ♘e3 ♘f4 36 ♘d5 ♘h5 37 ♘e3 ♗d8 38 ♘d5 ♘e6 39 ♔g1 ♘ef4 40 ♗c1 ♘xd5 41 ♖xd5 ♗b6+ 42 ♔h2 f6

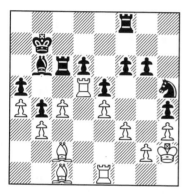

43 ♗e3?

Leaving himself with a really bad bishop. Even after this White should be able to hold the game, but it starts to become very unpleasant. And Petrosian maximizes the pain by being very patient, trying out different positions for his pieces before attempting any kind of breakthrough.

43...♗xe3 44 ♖xe3 ♖a8 45 ♔g1 ♘f4 46 ♖d2 ♘e6 47 ♖ed3 ♘d4 48 ♔f1 ♖f8 49 ♔f2 ♔c7 50 ♔f1 ♔d7 51 ♔f2 ♔e7 52 ♔f1 ♖a6 53 ♔f2 ♘e6 54 ♖e3 ♘c5 55 ♖d5 ♖aa8 56 ♔f1 ♘e6 57 ♖d2 ♘f4 58

♖e1 ♖a7 59 ♖ed1 ♖d7 60 ♖e1 ♖h8 61 ♖ed1 ♘e6 62 ♖e1 ♘d4 63 ♖ed1 ♔d8 64 ♖e1 ♔c7 65 ♖ed1 ♔c6 66 ♖e1 ♔c5 67 ♖e3 f5 68 ♔f2 ♖h5 69 ♔f1 ♖g5 70 ♔f2 ♖g3 71 ♔f1 ♖f7 72 ♔f2 ♖f8 73 ♔f1 ♖h8 74 ♔f2 ♖h5 75 ♔f1?

75 ♔g1 was necessary so as to meet 75...♖hg5 with 76 ♔h2. It's difficult to see how Black could then win.

75...♖hg5 76 ♖f2 ♔c6 77 ♖d2 ♔c7 78 ♖f2 ♘e6 79 ♖ee2 ♘f4

Threatening ...♘xh3.

80 ♖d2 ♔c6

Zugzwang. After 81 ♗d3 Black has 81...♘xd3 82 ♖xd3 fxe4, whilst 81 ♗b1 is met by 81...♘xh3 82 gxh3 ♖g1+ 83 ♔e2 ♖xb1 etc.

81 exf5 gxf5 82 ♗d1 ♖g7 83 ♗c2 ♖3g5 84 ♗d3 ♔d7 85 ♗c2 ♔e6 86 ♗d3 ♖g3 87 ♗c2 ♖g8 88 ♗d3

If 88 ♗b1 Black wins with 88...♘xh3.

88...e4! 89 fxe4 ♘xd3 90 ♖xf5 ♘c5 91 ♖fd5 ♖xb3 92 ♖xd6+ ♔e7 93 ♖6d4 ♖c3 94 e5 b3 95 ♗xh4 ♖c1+ 96 ♔f2 b2 0-1

8) Overcome the fear of losing

"Like everyone else, you want to learn the way to win. But never accept the way to lose. To accept defeat – to learn to die – is to be liberated from it. Once you accept, you are free to flow and to harmonize. Fluidity is the way to an empty mind. You must free your ambitious mind and learn the art of dying."

Bruce Lee

Defeat in chess can be likened to a symbolic death. Whilst most players can learn to take it in their stride, at the time of the game a player should feel that he's literally fighting for his life. Not to do so means that they are not as involved as they should be.

So how does someone reconcile the fear of a chessboard death with taking the necessary risks to win? Many players do not; for example, they'll withdraw themselves from the chess act so as not to feel too much pain when they lose. Such players are likely to dismiss their defeats by saying 'it's only a game'. But this leads to a dramatic lowering of motivation.

Other players may have their psyches more fully invested but then try to reduce the risk of ever losing. So whilst their motivation may be much stronger than those who don't care, they are likely to avoid moves which lead to strategic imbalance. This in turn may make it difficult for them to win games and thus enjoy much success in tournaments.

Is there a better way? Yes indeed, but it's not at all easy. The trick is to overcome the fear of losing without starting not to care, which in a sense means learning to die. This is something I've struggled with in my own game and I still draw far too many games. But I continue to find inspiration amongst some of the great players in history, such as the fearless Danish Grandmaster, Bent Larsen.

Larsen's remarkable tournament record was at least partially down to his willingness to risk losing. He saw a draw as the loss of half a point and would go out of his way to unbalance the game with risky openings. Here's a good example of both the danger and opportunity presented by his approach, an opening that misfires completely and then a brilliant fight back from a lost position:

**Game 10
B.Larsen-T.Van Scheltinga
Beverwijk 1964
Bird's Opening**

1 f4 ♘f6 2 ♘f3 d5 3 e3 g6 4 ♗e2 ♗g7 5 0-0 0-0 6 d3 b6 7 a4 ♗b7 8 ♕e1 c5 9 ♘bd2

This gets White's position into something of a tangle. A better follow-up to 7 a4 was 9 ♘a3.

9...♘c6 10 ♕h4 e6 11 ♖f2 ♘b4 12 ♘e1 ♘e8 13 ♕h3 ♘d6 14 g4 f5

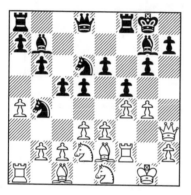

Black's prospects are already very good so Larsen changes the character of the position by setting up a 'Stonewall' formation.

15 gxf5 exf5 16 ♘df3 ♘f7 17 c3 ♘c6 18 d4 ♘a5

White would now prefer to have his a-pawn back on a2! This is a sure sign that things aren't going quite as planned.

19 ♗d1 c4 20 ♘e5 ♘xe5 21 fxe5 ♘b3 22 ♗xb3

White does not want to give up his

'good' bishop, especially with the remaining one looking so passive. But as we will soon see there are some compensating factors, mainly in the fact that White has a central pawn majority.

22...cxb3 23 ♘g2 ♕g5 24 ♖f4 ♕e7 25 ♗d2 ♗a6 26 ♖h4!?

In his book of selected games Larsen remarked that this was very risky, but part of the problem is that Black is ready to bring his bishop on a6 to d3 and then e4. This makes the need to take action rather more urgent.

26...g5! 27 ♖xh7 ♗e2!

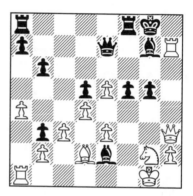

This is probably just winning for Black, the immediate threat being 27...♗g4!. But as we will soon see, winning this 'won' game against Larsen will not prove to be easy.

28 c4!!

A brilliant pawn sacrifice to activate the bishop on d2.

After 28 ♕h6 Black would play 28...♕f7 after which 29 e6 ♗xh6 30 ♖xf7 ♖xf7 31 exf7+ ♔xf7 leads to a clear advantage for Black in the endgame.

28...♗xc4

After 28...dxc4 White can play 29

♗c3 when White has two connected passed pawns and the bishop suddenly looks very strong.

Larsen was more concerned about 28...♖ac8, giving the line 29 cxd5 (29 e4 seems just bad after 29...fxe4 because of Black's threats along the f-file) 29...♖c2 30 ♗c3 ♖xc3!. But it seems that this is not so clear: for example, 31 bxc3 ♗d3 32 ♖e1 b2 33 ♖h5 g4 (33...b1♕ gives White more than enough for the piece after 34 ♖xb1 ♗xb1 35 d6 ♕d8 36 ♕g3 g4 37 e6 etc) 34 ♕h4 ♕a3 35 ♖g5 ♕xc3 36 ♖xg7+ ♔xg7 37 ♕g5+ with a draw by perpetual check.

29 ♘f4!!

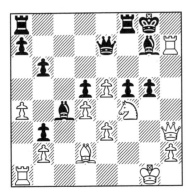

This astonishing follow-up suddenly turns the tables. There's little choice but to take the knight.

29...gxf4 30 ♔f2!

Threatening 31 ♖g1.

30...fxe3+ 31 ♗xe3 f4

After 31...♗d3 White wins with 32 ♗h6! ♔xh7 33 ♗g5+ etc.

32 ♗d2 ♔f7

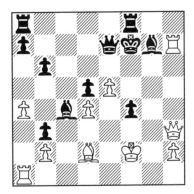

The last chance to make a fight of it was with 32...♕g5 33 ♖g1 ♕xg1+.

33 ♕h5+ ♔e6 34 ♕g4+ 1-0

An amazing 'swindle'.

9) Know yourself

"True mastery transcends any particular art. It stems from mastery of oneself – the ability, developed through self-discipline to be calm, fully aware, and completely in tune with oneself and the surroundings. Then, and only then, can a person know himself."

Bruce Lee

One of the most common problems amongst players who come to me for lessons is that they want to play like Mikhail Tal. Occasionally, very occasionally, this is an appropriate style for someone to adopt. Usually it is not.

Being ruthlessly objective about one's capabilities is one of the most valuable traits a chess player can have and it is simultaneously cultivated by playing the game. The chessboard has a way of ferreting out all of our weaknesses from vanity to pride and sloth. One of the signs of great players is that they are highly objective about both weaknesses and strengths. Here, for example, is a passage from *The Middle Years of Paul Keres* in which the great Estonian Grandmaster describes how he learned to conserve his energy by not playing too much. Such thoughts are typical of those who devote their lives to mastery:

"It is often said in the earliest part of my career that I conducted single, decisive games with an insufficient sense of responsibility and earnestness. But my participation in the training tournament at Leningrad and Moscow showed that such was also the case with me in whole events. It was naturally my desire to make acquaintance with the chess-masters of the Soviet Union and measure my strength with them over the board and, finally, to get to know their method of play and their various researches into the game of chess. But I should not in any way have undertaken this in the sort of form I found myself after the AVRO Tournament. I should have copied the example of Botvinnik who quite rightly refrained from taking part in this training tournament.

"Naturally, the consequences of this thoughtless behaviour on my part were not long in coming, especially when one takes into consideration the good playing calibre of the tournament participants. I lost two games in the very first rounds and had to make a vastly concentrated effort in order not to collapse completely. I succeeded in winning three good games in the middle part of the tournament, these being a highly complicated struggle against Tolush, one with an interesting exchange sacrifice against Levenfish and a well carried out King-side attack against Smyslov. But in a whole series of games I conducted play in a style beneath criticism, as for example in easily won endgames against Reshevsky and

Rabinowitsch, or in the encounter in the last round with Alatortsev. I stood well for quite a long time, but in the end my physical reserves were exhausted. I lost both of the last two games and finished up in the lower half of the table.

"The result of this tournament was indeed bitter for me, but also extremely instructive. Shortly after the Leningrad-Moscow Tournament I was invited to take part in a fine international tournament in Kemeri, but this time I did not repeat my mistake. I refrained from participating and only took part in national matches against Latvia and Lithuania. The next tournament in which I took part was some months later, the Easter Tournament at Margate. This time I was fresh once again, played very good chess and won the first prize, one point ahead of Capablanca and Flohr."

The following game is an example of the same thing. During an open tournament with some double-round days it makes sense for more mature players to play a tight, cautious game and not take too many risks. But in the following encounter Mark Taimanov paid insufficient heed to such considerations and I managed to beat him.

Game 11
M.Taimanov-N.Davies
Gausdal 1992
Nimzowitsch-Larsen Attack

---

1 ♘f3 ♘f6 2 b3 d5 3 ♗b2 c6 4 e3 ♗g4 5 h3 ♗xf3 6 ♕xf3 ♘bd7 7 g4!?

This is not the way that a man of over 60 years of age should be playing.

Although it might be a good move from an objective point of view, the loosening of White's position exposes him to greater risk. Where, for example, will White's king find safety?

7...e5 8 g5 ♘e4 9 h4 ♗b4!?

Fast and direct development is often a good response to an opponent's exotic play. In addition to pinning White's d-pawn, this provokes a weakening of his queenside with a2-a3.

10 ♗h3 ♕e7

I would have liked to have played another natural move in 10...0-0 but then 11 ♕f5! ♘b6 12 f3 ♘d6 13 ♕xe5 is very strong. Consequently I decide to force White into taking the knight on d7 in order to get the e5-pawn.

11 ♗xd7+ ♕xd7 12 ♗xe5 0-0

Black wants to play along the e- and f-files. What started out as a quiet Nimzowitsch Attack has been transformed into something more closely resembling a King's or Blackmar-Diemer Gambit.

13 a3 ♗a5 14 b4 ♗c7 15 ♗xc7 ♕xc7

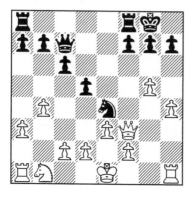

16 ♕f4?

The position was already looking scary for White, but after this it becomes downright bad. His extra pawn becomes worthless and Black still has a powerful initiative.

The best was probably 16 ♘c3 when 16...♘xc3 17 dxc3 ♕e5 18 ♔d2 f6 19 g6 hxg6 20 h5 seems fairly level in the endgame.

16...♕xf4 17 exf4 ♖ae8 18 ♔f1 f6 19 d3 ♘d6 20 ♘c3 fxg5 21 fxg5 ♘f5

The knight is en route for the d4-square from where it ties White down completely.

22 ♔g2 ♘d4 23 ♖ac1 ♖f4 24 ♔f1

24 ♘d1 ♖e2 25 c3 ♘f5 is hardly better.

24...♖ef8 25 ♘d1

If 25 ♖h2 then 25...♘f3 would win the pawn back with an ongoing initiative.

25...♘f5 26 ♖h3 ♘xh4 27 c4

Desperately trying to activate his rook on c1, but Black's reply prevents

this while simultaneously depriving White's knight of the e3-square.

27...d4 28 ♖c2 ♘f3 29 ♖e2 ♖g4 30 ♖h1 ♖f5

Threatening 31...♖fxg5 followed by 32...♖g1+. This prompts further desperation.

31 g6 ♖xg6 32 ♘b2 ♔f7 33 c5 ♖fg5 34 ♖c2 ♖e6 35 ♖e2 ♖h6 0-1

White can't take on h6 because of 36...♖g1 mate.

Taimanov, like Keres, seemed to learn from the experience; several years later he played in a tournament I helped to organize in Wrexham in North Wales and won the classiest victory with technique and restraint. It seemed as if he'd made an inventory of his strengths and weaknesses and looked to compensate for his age by keeping the games fairly stable.

Taimanov's best game in this tournament was the following encounter with the American International Master John Donaldson. It could equally have been included in the section on attacking two weaknesses.

<hr>

Game 12
J.Donaldson-M.Taimanov
Owens Corning,
Wrexham 1997
Bogo-Indian Defence

1 d4 ♘f6 2 c4 e6 3 ♘f3 ♗b4+ 4 ♗d2 a5 5 g3 d5 6 ♕c2 ♘c6

This is a system Taimanov has played for years so Donaldson must have been prepared for it. In fact he probably stands slightly better in the early stages.

7 a3 ♗e7 8 ♗g2 0-0 9 0-0 ♗d7 10 ♖d1 a4

An important move which stymies White's efforts to make progress on the queenside. Later in the game Taimanov will use the a-file to great effect.

11 cxd5 exd5 12 ♘c3 ♘a5 13 ♗g5 ♘b3 14 ♖ab1 ♖a5!

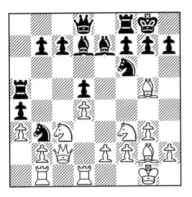

An original way to defend the d5-pawn and simultaneously activate the rook.

15 ♘e5 ♗e8 16 e3 h6 17 ♗xf6 ♗xf6 18 ♘d3 ♗c6 19 ♘b4 ♕d7 20 ♘ca2 ♗e7 21

♘c1?!

The start of a dubious plan: White believes that the doubled b-pawn position he is aiming for will be fine for him but he will be proved wrong.

White should have played something like 21 h4 envisaging 22 ♗f3 and 23 ♔g2.

21...♘xc1 22 ♖dxc1?

It was not too late to bail out with 22 ♘xc6 after which 22...♕xc6 23 ♕xc1 (23 ♕xc6 ♘e2+ 24 ♔f1 ♘xg3+ 25 hxg3 bxc6 would also be fine for Black) 23...♕xc1 24 ♖dxc1 c6 looks equal and drawish.

22...♗xb4 23 axb4 ♖a6 24 ♕c5 ♖b6!

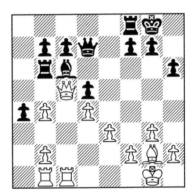

The contours of the coming endgame begin to emerge. Black's rook comes to the b-file in order to pressurize White's doubled and isolated b-pawns. And its colleague will join in later.

25 ♗f1?! ♗b5! 26 ♕xc7 ♕xc7 27 ♖xc7 ♗xf1 28 ♔xf1 ♖xb4

Reaching an endgame in which Black has all the chances. The first problem White faces is the passivity of his rooks which get tied down to the defence of his b2-pawn. If this were to fall, Black would obtain two connected passed pawns on the queenside.

29 ♖a1 ♖a8! 30 ♖a2 ♖a5!

Echoing Black's 14th move. The rook is headed for b5 from where it defends d5 and attacks b2.

31 ♔e2

After 31 ♖c5 ♖xc5 32 dxc5 ♔f8, Black's king would be en route for the c6-square from where it could pick up the c5-pawn.

31...♖ab5 32 ♖c8+ ♔h7 33 ♖c2 ♔g6 34 ♔d2

This plan of bringing the king to the queenside doesn't work. It might have been better to put it on f3 and then wait.

34...♔f5 35 f3 h5 36 ♔c1

This also looks wrong because now Black breaks up White's kingside pawns. 36 h3 looks better so as to meet 36...g5 with 37 g4+.

36...g5 37 ♖c7 f6 38 h3

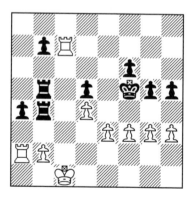

38...g4!

Drilling a hole into White's kingside pawn structure, after which Black's king can get in.

39 fxg4+ hxg4 40 h4

With White having set up his own passed pawn, the game finally sharpens. But with Taimanov having preserved his nervous energy with some sedate positional play, he handles the final stages better than his much younger opponent.

40...♔e4! 41 ♖e7+ ♔f3 42 h5 ♖b6 43 ♖a3

After 43 h6 Black would get his rook behind the passed pawn with 43...f5 44 h7 ♖h6 etc.

43...♔xg3 44 e4+ ♔f4 45 exd5 ♖c4+ 46 ♔b1 ♖xd4?!

The only slip in an otherwise excellent game. Black should have played 46...f5, advancing his passed pawns and stopping White's h-pawn in its tracks.

47 h6 f5 48 ♖e6 ♖b5

49 ♖h3?

Ingenious but bad. 49 h7 would have still made a game of it.

49...♖d2

And not 49...gxh3 because of 50 h7 etc.

50 h7 ♖bxb2+ 51 ♔c1?

Making it easy for Black. 51 ♔a1 had to be tried.

51...♖dc2+ 52 ♔d1 ♖h2!

The point. Threatened with 53...♖b1 mate, White has to exchange rooks.

53 ♖xh2 ♖xh2 54 ♖e7 g3 55 ♖g7 g2 0-1

After 56 ♖xg2 ♖xh7 Black would use his new passed pawn duo on b7 and a4.

How should someone go about performing such an inventory? The most vital ingredient is self-honesty, and because of this it makes sense to solicit the opinion of a strong player and instruct him not to spare your feelings. Once an accurate diagnosis has been made, the odds of finding effective medication improve considerably.

10) Healthy body, healthy mind

"Above all else, before playing in competitions a player must have regard to his health, for if he is suffering from ill-health he cannot hope for success."

Mikhail Botvinnik

Being physically fit for competitive chess was vital even in Botvinnik's day. So how much more true is it going to be in this day and age with the possibility of a non-stop seven-hour session. I believe that this increased intensity is a major reason why the average age of top players has diminished.

Being fit for competitive chess means having the stamina to concentrate over a long playing session and indeed the duration of a tournament. It stands to reason that if someone is ill or in poor physical condition their ability to do this will be diminished. Indeed there have been several players whose bohemian habits adversely affected their careers, most notably Mikhail Tal.

Tal was probably the most gifted player in chess history but his lifestyle led to frequent hospitalization for kidney problems. His greatest achievement came in 1960 when he defeated Botvinnik in a match for the World title. Yet he lost the return match the following year and was hospitalized during the 1962 Candidates tournament in Curacao. Here is one of his games from this event, where he is beaten by the underdog Pal Benko.

Game 13
P.Benko-M.Tal
Candidates Tournament,
Curacao 1962
Pirc Defence

---

1 g3 g6 2 ♗g2 ♗g7 3 d4 d6 4 e4 ♘f6 5 ♘e2 0-0 6 0-0 ♘bd7

The immediate 6...e5 is probably a more precise move, though Tal might have wanted to avoid a possible exchange of queens (via 7 dxe5) against a player with a liking of endgames. Unfortunately he finds himself ending up in a rather passive position.

7 ♘bc3 c6 8 a4 a5 9 b3 ♖e8 10 ♗a3 ♕c7 11 ♕d2 e5 12 ♖ad1 exd4 13 ♘xd4 ♘c5 14 f3 b6 15 ♘de2

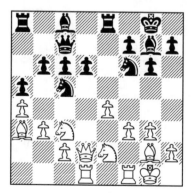

This position is not easy for Black because of the weakness of the backward d6-pawn and his lack of space. There is an analogous type of position in the King's Indian Defence in which White has a pawn on c4 rather than a4, but those tend to be a bit easier for Black to play.

15...♗f8 16 ♗b2 ♕e7 17 ♘d4 ♗b7 18 ♖fe1 ♗g7 19 f4

White methodically strengthens his position whereas Black has difficulty finding an active plan. Not a pleasant situation for the dynamic Tal.

19...♖ad8 20 ♗f3 ♕d7 21 ♕g2 d5?!

The first sign that Black is losing patience.

22 e5 ♘fe4 23 ♘xe4 dxe4 24 ♗e2

Of course the pawn is temporarily immune because of 24 ♗xe4 ♘xe4 25 ♕xe4 c5 etc. But that does not mean it will be immune for ever.

24...♕e7 25 ♗a3 f6?

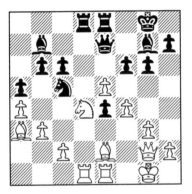

When someone is ill they can lack patience. This attempt to break free from White's bind opens the floodgates.

26 ♗c4+ ♔h8 27 ♘e6 ♖d5

Tal no doubt intended this exchange sacrifice, possibly as a means of exploiting Benko's habitual time trouble. Unfortunately it proves too easy for White to refute.

28 ♗xd5 cxd5 29 ♘xg7 ♔xg7 30 exf6+ ♕xf6 31 ♕f2

31 ♗xc5 bxc5 would actually give Black very nice compensation because of his central pawns and the potential pressure on the a8-h1 diagonal. Of course White is not easily going to give up his blockade of the dark squares.

31...♘e6 32 ♕xb6 ♗a8 33 ♗d6

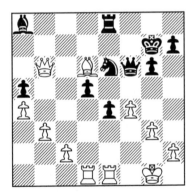

All White has to do now is reach the time control without being mated on g2.

33...♕f5 34 ♕xa5 ♔h6 35 c4 ♖d8 36 ♗e7 e3 37 ♖xe3 ♖e8 38 ♗g5+ ♔g7 39 ♖de1 ♘xg5 40 fxg5 ♖f8 41 ♕a7+ 1-0

A link between health and competitive chess is hardly surprising, but there may also be more subtle connections between body and mind. In the book *Descartes' Error* by Antonio Damasio, the author, a neuroscientist, challenges traditional ideas on what constitutes someone's 'mind'. Here's an excerpt:

"The idea that the mind derives from the entire organism as an ensemble may sound counterintuitive at first. Of late, the concept of mind has moved from the ethereal nowhere place it occupied in the seventeenth century to its current residence in or around the brain – a bit of a demotion, but still a dignified station. To suggest that the mind itself depends on brain-body interactions, in terms of evolutionary biology, ontogeny (individual development), and current operation may seem too much. But stay with me. What I am suggesting is that the mind arises from activity in neural circuits, to be sure, but many of those circuits were shaped in evolution by functional requisites of the organism, and that a normal mind will happen only if those circuits represent the organism continuously, as it is perturbed by stimuli from the physical and sociocultural environments and as it acts on those environments. If the basic topic of those representations were not an organism anchored in the body, we might have some form of mind, but I doubt that it would be the mind we do have.

"I am not saying that the mind is in the body. I am saying that the body contributes more than life support and modulatory effects to the brain. It contributes a content that is part and parcel of the workings of the normal mind."

Damasio's ideas certainly make sense to me. Indeed, in analysing the games of hundreds of players I've often sensed that certain imbalances in their play have been related to some aspect of their physical condition, such as obesity or being on medication. Future research will hopefully shed more light on such phenomenon. For now it seems reasonable that one should be as healthy as possible if only because of the stamina issue.

Chapter Two

Preparation

"The one who figures on victory at headquarters before even doing battle is the one who has the most strategic factors on his side."

Sun Tzu (*The Art of War*)

The eve of battle tends to require a different set of guidelines to those required for the general cultivation of someone's game. If they value the outcome a tournament or match can present a new set of pressures, particular opponents may well be known, the environment can be unfamiliar. All of these things need to be borne in mind if one wishes to maximize the odds of success.

How should someone prepare for a game? To a large extent this is a personal matter; strong players tend to develop their own individual approach over time. What I have found most useful is to make sure I am fit for battle so as to diminish tiredness and lapses of concentration that can result in disaster. Consideration of the opponent tends to come second, and here I'll try to understand what makes them tick. I might look over a few of their games but will never spend more than 30-40 minutes doing so. More than this tends to be counterproductive in that it contributes towards tiredness and fills the mind with concern.

11) Sleep well

*"Sleep deprivation can also affect your performance by reducing cognitive ability –
your ability to think and use your brain. Combined with drowsiness, this can greatly increase the risk of accidents because you're less able or quick at thinking your way fast out
of a dangerous problem.*

*"Along with the delays and errors in doing mental tasks, there's a slowing down of men-
tal arithmetic and logical reasoning. Memory is affected by sleep deprivation, with reduced
immediate recall, although information acquired before sleep deprivation is normal.*

*"Although it reduces the ability to do simple or monotonous tasks, ones which need
more attention and effort aren't so badly affected. Attention and concentration can drag a
tired brain into action. However, certain aspects of these complex tasks are affected, particularly the ability to think laterally."*

Dr Trisha Macnair

Proper sleep is vital for the brain to function well, but it's amazing how many
players neglect it. Meeting up with friends at a tournament often leads to over-
enthusiastic socializing in which many players stay in the bar until the early hours
of the morning. This has a double whammy effect: not only does the sleep deprivation cause a loss of brain function but the alcohol diminishes the quality of any
sleep that's been had.

Of course many amateur players do see tournaments and matches as part of
their social life and will risk downgrading their abilities as long as they have a
'good time'. This is a valid choice and I can understand people making it. They
just shouldn't make it without a full realization of the potential damage they're
doing to their performance.

If someone is staying away from home there are other issues too. Many people
tend not to sleep as well in an alien environment and hotels can also be noisy. For
these reasons it's good to choose your accommodation thoughtfully and taking
precautions such as requesting a quiet room and maybe bringing ear plugs.
Should someone sleep badly away from home there's also a case for some kind of
soporific, but research should be done to make sure there are no side effects such
as ongoing drowsiness.

The following game was played in the tournament in which I made my first
Grandmaster norm, Oslo 1988. The evening before the game most of the participants went out to a jazz bar, which is something I'd never do now. But I knew

who my opponent would be the following day and made sure that I drank less than he did and retired earlier. It turns out that I was in better shape for the mortal combat that followed:

Game 14
E.Gausel-N.Davies
Oslo 1988
Modern Defence

1 d4 d6 2 e4 g6 3 ♘c3 ♗g7 4 ♗c4 ♘c6 5 ♗e3 ♘f6 6 h3

This prevents Black's idea of 6...♘g4 but loses time. White should probably have played 5 ♘f3 when 5...♘f6 would have transposed into a Pirc Defence.

6...e5 7 dxe5

And here 7 ♘f3 would have avoided any further loss of time.

7...♘xe5 8 ♗b3 0-0 9 ♕d2

White was evidently not at his best in this game, the text being a further inaccuracy after which Black gets to take the initiative. 9 ♘f3 followed by castling kingside would have been a more sober approach.

9...b5!

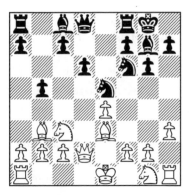

This flanking blow often appears in such positions; see for example my game as Black against Godena. If White takes on b5 then the important e4-pawn falls.

10 f3 b4 11 ♘d5 ♘xd5 12 ♗xd5 c6 13 ♗b3 a5 14 a4 d5

Opening the centre whilst White's king is still there.

15 exd5

Running to the queenside with 15 0-0-0 would not help as there would follow 15...♕f6 16 ♗d4 c5!, driving the bishop from its defence of b2.

15...♘c4! 16 ♗xc4 ♗xb2

Putting White in terrible trouble because of the threats of 17...♗xa1, 17...♗c3 and 17...♕h4+.

17 ♘e2

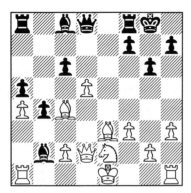

17...♕h4+

This is even stronger than taking the rook which now has to lose time evading capture.

18 ♗f2 ♕xc4 19 ♖b1 ♗c3 20 ♘xc3 bxc3

21 ♕d3 ♖e8+ 22 ♔d1

22 ♔f1 ♕xd3+ 23 cxd3 ♗f5 would prolong White's agony.

22...♕a2 23 ♖c1 ♗a6 24 ♕xc3 ♕xd5+ 25 ♕d2 ♖ad8 0-1

The final position is quite picturesque, assuming one is not on the receiving end.

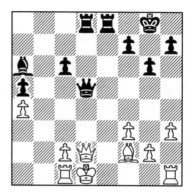

12) Eat breakfast

"Breakfast is one of the most important meals of the day because of its direct impact on the mental (and physical) performance in the morning. It has a direct effect on the glucose concentration in the brain and liver, and supplies a number of nutrients which are essentials to produce neurotransmitters, chemical messengers which act over neuronal cells communications.

"Many investigations have shown that mental concentration can be affected when doing intellectual activities in the morning without having had breakfast previously, and that a proper breakfast helps to keep the mental performance in that moment of the day, according to tests on memory and attention. Even if specific investigations are still necessary for chess on this matter, it can be inferred that the performance of chess players who train or compete during the morning hours could be affected in the same way."

Roberto H. Baglione (*Nutritional Practices of Chess Grandmasters*)

As with getting enough sleep this seems an obvious enough rule to follow. Yet once again it's something that many players ignore, often for the same reason of late socializing. By the time they wake up in the morning the hotel kitchen has closed or they simply do not have enough time to eat it before the game starts. In either case their ability to concentrate can suffer.

What's the best kind of food to eat during a tournament? Probably it's better to avoid fatty foods or red meat before a game as they will cause blood to go to the stomach. It is better to choose from fish, grains, salad and vegetables and not overdo it.

Another food related issue is that of being overweight. Does this have an effect on someone's chess? The fact that this may also be associated with a lack of fitness and stamina can, I believe, lead to certain imbalances in a player's style. For example, a player may learn to try and avoid long games after recognizing that he becomes tired and may make lazy 'natural' moves when he should be calculating variations.

I've noticed this tendency in many overweight players and it even seems to affect the greats. Efim Bogoljubow was one very large Grandmaster and his style of play was a kind of flowing aggression. This could of course work wonderfully well against lesser lights but proved less effective against the likes of Capablanca.

Game 15
J.Capablanca-E.Bogoljubow
BCF Congress, London 1922
Ruy Lopez

---

1 e4 e5

I suspect that had Bogoljubow been born 80 years later, he would have adopted the Sicilian Defence with 1...c5. But in 1922 it was neither very popular nor respectable.

2 ♘f3 ♘c6 3 ♗b5 a6 4 ♗a4 ♘f6 5 0-0 ♗e7 6 ♖e1 b5 7 ♗b3 d6 8 c3 0-0 9 d4 exd4 10 cxd4 ♗g4 11 ♗e3

White might have tried to exploit Black's move order (9...cxd4 10 cxd4 ♗g4 rather than 9...♗g4) by playing 11 ♘c3, after which 11...♗xf3 12 gxf3 leaves Black struggling against White's powerful centre and two bishops.

11...♘a5 12 ♗c2 ♘c4 13 ♗c1 c5 14 b3 ♘a5 15 ♗b2 ♘c6 16 d5 ♘b4 17 ♘bd2 ♘xc2 18 ♕xc2 ♖e8 19 ♕d3 h6 20 ♘f1 ♘d7 21 h3

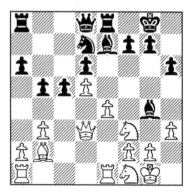

21...♗h5

Although this move was criticized

at the time, I think that Black lost this game much later on. Admittedly he would not have stood badly after 21...♗xf3 22 ♕xf3 ♗f6 either.

22 ♘3d2

Preparing to shut Black's light-squared bishop out of the game with a later g2-g4 and even f2-f4.

22...♗f6 23 ♗xf6 ♕xf6 24 a4

Although it has never been fashionable to criticize Capablanca's moves, I'm not sure this is right.

The immediate 24 ♕e3 could have been met by 24...g5 preventing f2-f4, but 24 ♘g3 ♗g6 25 ♕e3 intending 26 f4 looks fine for White.

24...c4! 25 bxc4 ♘c5 26 ♕e3 bxa4 27 f4 ♕e7 28 g4

After 28 f5 f6 Black creates a square for his bishop in the nick of time. So Capablanca opts for shutting it out of play.

28...♗g6 29 f5 ♗h7 30 ♘g3 ♕e5 31 ♔g2 ♖ab8 32 ♖ab1

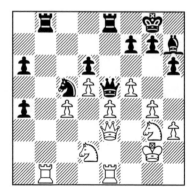

32...f6?!

This is exactly the kind of thing I mentioned earlier; Black plays a natural 'flowing' move when he should have been thinking in more concrete terms.

The right move is 32...♖b2 when the position is not easy for White. I think he should play 33 ♖xb2 (33 ♖e2 ♖xb1 34 ♘xb1 ♖b8 is better for Black) 33...♕xb2 34 ♖b1. For example, 34...♕c2 35 ♘e2 ♘b3 36 ♖xb3! axb3 37 ♘d4 ♕a2 38 ♘4xb3 a5 39 ♕c3 ♖b8 40 ♕xa5 leads to what is probably a drawn endgame.

33 ♘f3 ♖b2+ 34 ♖xb2 ♕xb2+ 35 ♖e2 ♕b3 36 ♘d4 ♕xe3 37 ♖xe3 ♖b8 38 ♖c3 ♔f7 39 ♔f3 ♖b2 40 ♘ge2 ♗g8 41 ♘e6

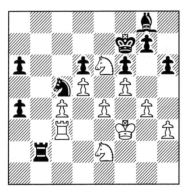

41...♘b3?!

Once again this is the natural move, and once again it is dubious.

41...♔e7 is far from obvious but seems to hold. For example, 42 ♘xg7 (or 42 ♘xc5 dxc5 43 ♔e3 ♗f7 44 ♘f4

♔d6) 42...♘b3 43 ♔e3 a3 44 ♘c1 ♖b1 45 ♘a2 ♖h1 46 ♔f4 ♖f1+ 47 ♔e3 ♖h1 draws by repetition.

It also seems as if 41...♘xe4 is a better try, and here 42 ♔xe4 ♖xe2+ 43 ♔d4 ♖d2+ 44 ♖d3 ♖xd3+ 45 ♔xd3 ♗h7 46 ♔c3 g6 finally gets the bishop working again.

42 c5 dxc5 43 ♘xc5 ♘d2+ 44 ♔f2 ♔e7 45 ♔e1! ♘b1 46 ♖d3

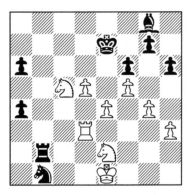

Only now does it become clear that White is on top, and here a blunder by a tired Bogoljubow decides matters.

46...a3??

46...♔d6 47 ♘xa4 ♖b4 48 ♘ac3 ♘xc3 49 ♘xc3 ♗f7 would still put up a fight.

47 d6+ ♔d8 48 ♘d4 ♖b6 49 ♘de6+ ♗xe6 50 fxe6 ♖b8 51 e7+ ♔e8 52 ♘xa6 1-0

13) Know your opponent

"Against a machine strategic psychology is very important. In certain positions, generally open positions, computer programs can be unbelievably strong. But they are also very weak in positions where they cannot see a plan. To play a machine, you have to limit its unlimited potential to find combinations and to threaten your king or other pieces. I tried to select openings where the machine didn't have a clear plan."

Garry Kasparov after beating Deep Blue in 1996.

In this age of computer databases and deep openings analysis, preparation has played an ever greater role in top tournaments. And with ever more games finding their way onto these databases even club level players can look their opponents' games up before they play them.

How should someone prepare for a game in which they know their opponent? For many players it's a question of looking up the openings their opponents play and reminding themselves about what they should do against them. The problem with this approach is that if this opponent has a wide opening repertoire it can easily lead to pre-game exhaustion.

I think that a better method is to try to gain a general impression about someone's play, trying to get inside their heads and understand how they are likely to react in different situations. So for players who appear to be comfortable with the initiative it might be a good idea to deprive them of it, whereas against those who prefer defence it is often a good idea to make them attack, either by snatching a hot pawn or inflicting some structural damage on their position. Of course it requires some experience to be able to read opponents in this way but it can be very rewarding.

If there is no time to prepare or you are unable to find any of your opponent's games there are still many things that can be learned at the board. If they arrive late, dishevelled and have forgotten to bring a pen with them this might imply a certain lack of organizational skills. If they make extensive markings on their score sheets you are probably facing a time trouble addict who is attempting to get on the wagon. Do they get up from the board after every move or just sit there and concentrate? All these things provide vital clues as to who you are facing and where their strengths and weaknesses may lie.

Computers are a good way to illustrate these issues because of their one-sided 'style' of play – highly tactical, having a strong tendency towards materialism but often being blind to long-term issues and strategies. David Bronstein once advised me that a good way to beat computers was to sacrifice a pawn, as it threw out their evaluation function. And in the following game he gives a beautiful demonstration of this strategy.

> ## Game 16
> ### D.Bronstein-
> ### Comp Mephisto Genius
> ### The Hague 1996
> *Pseudo Trompowsky*

1 d4 d5 2 &g5

One of the stages of the game in which intuition is more valuable than calculation is the opening. Unfortunately for humans there is also the issue that the opening moves have been well mapped out and that this web of variations can be 'remembered' perfectly by a machine. It follows that humans should try to avoid well-trodden paths.

2...c6 3 e3 &b6 4 &c1

Not giving the machine any material just yet.

4...&f5 5 &f3 &d7 6 &bd2 &gf6 7 c4 e6 8 c5

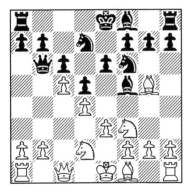

Whilst it is often a mistake to play this kind of move, in this particular position Black will find it difficult to get ...e6-e5 in. So White is able to maintain his space advantage.

8...&c7 9 b4 &e7

After 9...e5 White would be able to inflict some structural weaknesses with 10 dxe5 &xe5 11 &xf6 gxf6 12 &d4.

10 &b3 0-0 11 &f4 &d8 12 h3

Anticipating Black's 12...&h5. White wants to keep his dark-squared bishop.

12...&h5 13 &h2 &g6 14 &e2 &hf6 15 0-0 &e4 16 &a5 &c8 17 b5

Despite having played an innocuous-looking opening, White is clearly better now because of the weaknesses he's inflicting on Black's queenside.

17...&d8 18 bxc6 bxc6 19 &a3 &h5 20 g4!?

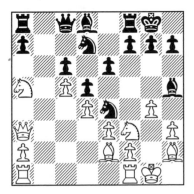

Black had the idea of playing 20...&xf3 followed by 21...&d2, but it's interesting that Bronstein played this rather than something like 20 &fc1.

Perhaps reasoning that computers underestimate the weakness of king positions he figured he would not be attacked.

20...♗g6 21 ♖ab1!?

Now Bronstein offers some material, Black's reply 'winning' either a pawn or the exchange. In either case he would get excellent compensation in return.

21...♘g5

A lot of humans would be inclined to play 21...f5, trying to soften up White's kingside.

22 ♖b2!?

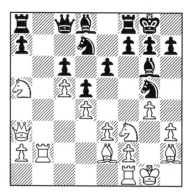

Another promising line is 22 ♘xg5 when 22...♗xb1 23 ♖xb1 ♗xg5 24 ♕a4 will win the pawn on c6 with more than enough compensation.

22...♘xh3+ 23 ♔g2 ♘g5 24 ♘xg5 ♗xg5 25 ♗d6

25 ♕a4 would also be quite strong.

25...♖e8 26 ♕a4 ♘b8

Black can no longer defend c6 but he does at least manage to get White to part with his powerful dark-squared bishop.

27 ♗xb8 ♖xb8 28 ♖xb8 ♕xb8 29 ♘xc6

♕c7 30 f4 ♖c8 31 ♘e5 ♗e4+ 32 ♗f3 ♗xf3+ 33 ♔xf3

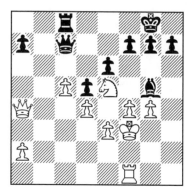

Despite moving towards the centre of the board, the king is quite safe here. In fact in an endgame it can even become very strong.

33...♗f6 34 ♘d3 g5

Trying to expose White's king whilst creating 'luft' for its own, but this does little to distract White from his plan of winning with the passed c-pawn. The next logical stage is to exchange queens.

35 ♖b1 gxf4 36 ♘xf4 ♗g5 37 ♕b5 ♖d8 38 ♕b7 ♖c8

38...♕a5 might have been a better practical try, aiming to take advantage of White's exposed king. Once queens are off the board Black's counterplay disappears.

39 ♕xc7 ♖xc7 40 ♖b8+ ♔g7 41 ♘h5+ ♔h6 42 a4

Threatening to advance the pawn to a6 and then play ♖b8-b7. Black tries desperately to wriggle free but it's rather too late.

42...f5 43 ♖e8 ♖c6 44 ♘f4 ♗xf4 45 ♔xf4 fxg4 46 ♖g8!

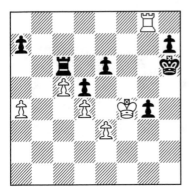

Here too we see Bronstein's computer-hostile strategy at work. He continues to throw out its assessments by using material imbalance and at the same time cuts Black's king off from the queenside.

46...♖a6 47 ♖xg4 ♖xa4

Despite Black's extra pawn the position is hopeless.

48 ♔e5 ♖a6 49 ♔f6 ♔h5 50 ♖g1 h6 51 ♖c1 ♖c6 52 ♔e7 1-0

14) Become the enemy

"*To* become the enemy *means to think yourself into the enemy's position. In the world people tend to think of a robber trapped in a house as a fortified enemy. However, if we think of becoming the enemy, we feel that the whole world is against us and that there is no escape. He who is shut inside is a pheasant. He who enters to arrest is a hawk. You must appreciate this.*

"*In large-scale strategy, people are always under the impression that the enemy is strong, and so tend to become cautious. But if you have good soldiers, and if you understand the principles of strategy, and if you know how to beat the enemy, there is nothing to worry about.*

"*In single combat you must put yourself in the enemy's position. If you think, 'Here is a master of the Way, who knows the principles of strategy', then you will surely lose. You must consider this deeply.*"

Myamoto Musashi (*The Book of Five Rings*)

Besides the issue of an opponent's style of play, it is useful to consider what he wants to do in a particular game. The obvious situation is when the state of a tournament or match requires that they try for either a win or a draw, with a special circumstance being when they need to make a certain result for a title norm. One can also guess their intentions if, for example, you are the lower-rated player and have Black; the odds are that they will be trying to beat you. It's less easy to judge if you are lower rated but have White or are higher rated but have Black. In this case much depends on the rating difference and just your opponent's attitude to draws. Bent Larsen always played for a win against everyone, and with either colour. Experience is a great help in learning to judge these things, and as Musashi would have said, you must consider this deeply.

The following game was the last of the 1987 match between Garry Kasparov and Anatoly Karpov, with Kasparov trailing his opponent by a point. Desperately needing a win to retain his title, Kasparov might have been expected to come out all guns blazing. Instead he produced a psychological masterpiece by putting himself in Karpov's position and realizing how difficult it would be for his opponent to play a long, drawn out game. There were points at which Karpov could indeed have drawn, but in the event the pressure proved too much for him.

Game 17
G.Kasparov-A.Karpov
World Championship
(24th game), Seville 1987
Réti Opening

---

1 c4

At first sight this seems like an astonishing decision for a 'must win' game, but Kasparov shows masterful judgement in his choice of opening. A long tense struggle is exactly the thing that will be most trying on Black's nerves.

1...e6 2 ♘f3 ♘f6 3 g3 d5 4 b3 ♗e7 5 ♗g2 0-0 6 0-0 b6 7 ♗b2 ♗b7 8 e3 ♘bd7 9 ♘c3 ♘e4

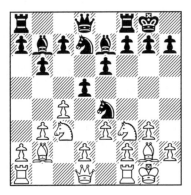

10 ♘e2!?

Keeping the tension by avoiding an exchange of knights.

10...a5 11 d3 ♗f6 12 ♕c2 ♗xb2 13 ♕xb2 ♘d6 14 cxd5 ♗xd5 15 d4! c5 16 ♖fd1 ♖c8?!

16...c4!? is probably a good move here but Karpov would have been reluctant to unbalance the position like this with so much at stake. After the move he makes in the game White gets bishop for knight and stands slightly better.

17 ♘f4 ♗xf3 18 ♗xf3 ♕e7 19 ♖ac1 ♖fd8 20 dxc5 ♘xc5

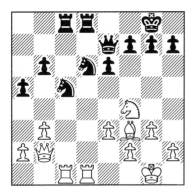

21 b4!

This exposes a Black weakness (the b6-pawn) along the b-file.

21...axb4 22 ♕xb4 ♕a7 23 a3 ♘f5 24 ♖b1 ♖xd1+ 25 ♖xd1 ♕c7 26 ♘d3! h6?!

Here 26...g6 was the right move.

27 ♖c1 ♘e7 28 ♕b5 ♘f5 29 a4 ♘d6 30 ♕b1 ♕a7 31 ♘e5!

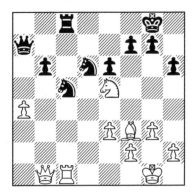

31...♘xa4?

According to Kasparov this should

---

have lost on the spot, though with both players in time trouble some further errors are about to appear.

After 31...♕xa4 Kasparov gave the long variation 32 ♕xb6 ♕a3! 33 ♖d1 ♘f5 34 ♖d8+ ♖xd8 35 ♕xd8+ ♔h7 36 ♘xf7 ♕c1+ 37 ♔g2 ♕b2! 38 e4 ♘e3+ 39 ♔h3 ♕xf2 40 ♕h8+ ♔g6 41 ♘e5+ ♔f6 42 ♕f8+ ♔xe5 43 ♕xc5+ ♔f6 44 ♕f8+ ♔e5 45 ♕xg7+ ♔d6 46 e5+ ♔c5 47 ♕f8+ ♔d4 48 ♕b4+ ♘c4 49 ♗g4 ♕f1+ 50 ♔h4 ♔xe5 51 ♕c5+ ♔e4 52 ♕c6+ winning the e6-pawn but maybe still not the game. Furthermore, Black could just decline the pawn with 31...♘f5!?.

32 ♖xc8+ ♘xc8 33 ♕d1?

Missing a chance in time trouble. In his notes to the game Kasparov gave the variation 33 ♕b5! ♔h7! (33...♘d6 is met by 34 ♕c6, and 33...♔f8 by 34 ♘c6 ♕a8 35 ♕d3! g6 36 ♕d4! threatening 37 ♕h8+ etc) 34 ♘c6 ♕a8 35 ♕d3+! f5 (35...g6 loses to 36 ♕d7 ♔g7 37 ♘e5) 36 ♕d8 (threatening 37 ♘e7) 36...♘c5 37 ♔g2 ♕a2 38 ♘e5! ♕b2 39 ♘f7 ♕f6 40 ♕h8+ ♔g6 41 ♕g8! with the decisive threat of 42 ♘h8+.

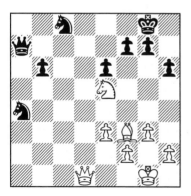

33...♘e7?

Black in turn misses the best defence. 33...♘c5! would have allowed Karpov to recover his title after 34 ♕d8+ ♔h7 35 ♔g2! f6! 36 ♘c6 ♕d7 etc.

34 ♕d8+ ♔h7 35 ♘xf7 ♘g6 36 ♕e8 ♕e7 37 ♕xa4 ♕xf7 38 ♗e4

Now it's clear that White is on top, but it's a long hard grind to a full point from here. Of course, as hard as it is for White to win it's even harder for Black to draw.

38...♔g8 39 ♕b5 ♘f8 40 ♕xb6 ♕f6 41 ♕b5 ♕e7 42 ♔g2 g6 43 ♕a5 ♕g7 44 ♕c5 ♕f7 45 h4 h5?

This is the wrong plan, as the g6- and h5-pawn duo is a target. 45...♔g7 would have been a better defence when it's still not clear that White can win.

46 ♕c6 ♕e7 47 ♗d3 ♕f7 48 ♕d6 ♔g7 49 e4 ♔g8 50 ♗c4 ♔g7 51 ♕e5+ ♔g8 52 ♕d6 ♔g7 53 ♗b5 ♔g8 54 ♗c6 ♕a7 55 ♕b4! ♕c7 56 ♕b7! ♕d8 57 e5!

The arrival of this pawn on e5 signals the beginning of the end.

57...♕a5

White now has a position in which he can afford to exchange queens, for example 57...♕d3 58 ♗e8 ♕f5 59 ♕f3! is winning. This makes all the difference.

58 ♗e8 ♕c5 59 ♕f7+ ♔h8 60 ♗a4 ♕d5+ 61 ♔h2 ♕c5 62 ♗b3 ♕c8 63 ♗d1 ♕c5 64 ♔g2 1-0

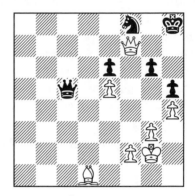

Karpov resigned to avoid further suffering, seeing that the position was now quite lost. After 64...♕b4 there would follow 65 ♗f3 ♕c5 66 ♗e4 ♕b4 67 f3! (White must avoid the stalemate trick 67 ♗xg6?? ♘xg6 68 ♕xg6 ♕b7+ 69 ♔h2 ♕g2+!! etc) 67...♕d2+ 68 ♔h3 ♕b4 69 ♗xg6 ♘xg6 70 ♕xg6 ♕xh4+ 71 ♔g2! and White wins.

15) Choose a favourable battleground

"So among military forces there are those who rush, those who tarry, those who fall, those who crumble, those who riot, and those who get beaten. These are not natural disasters, but faults of the generals.

"Those who have equal momentum but strike ten with one are in a rush. Those whose soldiers are strong but whose officers are weak tarry. Those whose officers are strong but whose soldiers are weak fall. When colonels are angry and obstreperous and fight on their own out of spite when they meet opponents, and the generals do not know their abilities, they crumble."

Sun Tzu (*The Art of War*)

Choosing the right battleground is an essential part of winning chess and should be done with regard to each player's abilities. Once a player understands an opponent's style and is able to gauge their intentions it becomes easier to choose a suitable battleground. To a large extent this will be the choice of opening but it can also depend on how someone plays an opening. Often there will be a choice of plans so consideration should be given to their efficacy against a particular opponent.

In the following game I played against a young and gifted opponent who evidently liked the initiative and to be able to force the pace. Accordingly I played an opening which was popular before he was born and managed to take him outside his comfort zone:

Game 18
N.Davies-L.D'Costa
British League 2007
King's Indian Attack

---

1 ♘f3 c5 2 e4 d6 3 c3

Naturally it never occurred to me to play 3 d4 against a talented young player with a good memory and an interest in the latest theory. Instead I opt for an opening I have played for some 35 years where experience and understanding is of greater value.

3...♘f6 4 g3

I like to play this only when Black has committed himself to putting his knight on f6. This is to sidestep some of Black's more effective set-ups.

4...♘c6 5 d3 g6 6 ♗g2 ♗g7 7 0-0 0-0 8 ♖e1 e5 9 ♘bd2

A year earlier in the same competition I had played 9 a3 against Sam Collins. That game continued 9...d5 10 ♘bd2 d4 11 cxd4 cxd4 12 b4 a6 13 ♘b3

♘e8 14 ♗g5 f6 15 ♗d2 ♘d6 when White had nothing special. This time round I played 9 ♘bd2 so that after 9...d5 I would get a reversed King's Indian Defence with not one but two extra tempi. Frankly I was astonished when Black played:

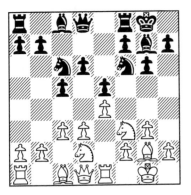

9...d5?

I saw from my opponent's games that he did not have any experience with the King's Indian. Perhaps this, coupled with the modern database search approach to preparation, explains this move.

10 exd5 ♘xd5 11 ♘c4 ♖e8 12 ♘g5!

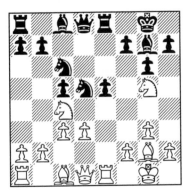

In the analogous King's Indian posi-

tion White would have played h2-h3 in order to stop Black's ...♘f6-g4. Here this knight move is very strong, setting up latent threats against f7 (via ♕d1-b3 on the next move) and preparing to bring the knight to e4 and then d6.

12...♖f8

Black sank into thought before playing this way; obviously things have gone horribly wrong already.

After 12...h6 White can play 13 ♘e4 ♗f8 14 ♘ed6. For example, 14...♗xd6 (14...♘xc3 15 bxc3 ♗xd6 16 ♗xh6 is also good for White) 15 ♗xd5 ♔g7 16 ♕d2 g5 17 h4 ♗e7 18 ♗xc6 bxc6 19 ♖xe5 winning a pawn.

13 ♕b3

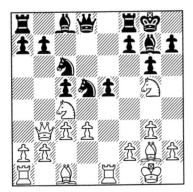

13...♘de7

Another possibility was 13...♘b6 when 14 ♗e3 would be unpleasant. Retreating the knight to e7 looks solid, but Black is conceding time and space. I decided it was time to open things up.

14 f4! exf4 15 ♗xf4 ♘d5

White can also meet 15...h6 with 16 ♘xf7: for example, 16...♖xf7 17 ♘d6 ♕f8 18 ♗xc6 bxc6 (if 18...♘xc6 there follows 19 ♘xf7 ♕xf7 20 ♖e8+ ♗f8 21

♗xh6) 19 ♘xf7 ♕xf7 20 ♖xe7 etc.

One other possibility is 15...♘f5, but then 16 ♘e4 b6 17 ♘xc5 is winning.

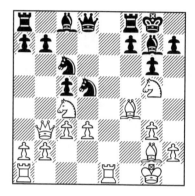

16 ♘xf7!

A devastating blow.

16...♖xf7 17 ♘d6 c4 18 ♕xc4 1-0

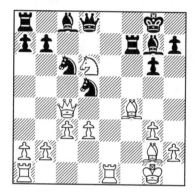

Black is losing back the piece with interest.

16) Focus on winning

"No matter if the enemy has thousands of men, there is fulfilment in simply standing them off and being determined to cut them down, starting from one end. You will finish the greater part of it."

Yamamoto Tsunetomo (*The Hagakure*)

One of the worst things a player can do is to go into the game with a negative, fearful attitude. It's much better for players to focus on winning, even if they are heavily out-rated.

The reason for this can be understood by looking at the motivation of both players. If someone plays passively and tries to exchange pieces they are not going to create much fear or doubt in the mind of their opponent, who will then be able to take all sorts of liberties with them. If, on the other hand, someone comes out fighting it can create a certain hesitancy in even the strongest and most confident of players.

In the following game it seemed to me that White was playing far too passively and this conceded the initiative. Later on he switched gears towards being rather too aggressive and this in turn precipitated his downfall.

Game 19
S.Conner-N.Davies
Liverpool League 2008
Sicilian Defence

---

1 e4 c5 2 ♘f3 e6 3 d4 cxd4 4 ♘xd4 a6 5 ♘c3 ♘e7

This is a move I've been experimenting with of late. Black may be getting ready to adopt the Taimanov plan with knights on e7 and c6, but he can also bring the e7-knight to c6. Although it looks rather strange and slow, the advantage of not putting a knight on f6 is that White cannot attack

it with a subsequent e4-e5.

6 g3 ♘bc6

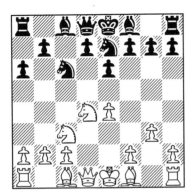

7 ♗g2

7 ♘b3 is a better move, giving Black the problem of where to put his knight

on e7. But it seems that White was happy to exchange pieces, perhaps because he thought this was his best chance for a draw.

7...♘xd4 8 ♕xd4 ♘c6 9 ♕d1 b5 10 0-0 ♗b7 11 ♗e3 ♗e7

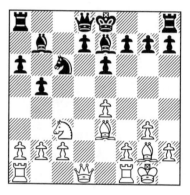

12 ♘e2?!

White wants to exchange the other knight by putting it on d4, thus confirming the suspicions I had after White's 7th move. The flaw in this idea is that I can move my knight away from c6.

12...0-0 13 ♘d4

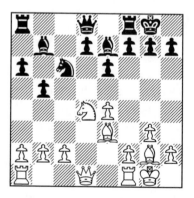

13...♘e5!

Avoiding the exchange and aiming

for the c4-square. White makes one last attempt to exchange it before switching to a rather more desperate approach.

14 ♘f3?

After Black's reply White is in all sorts of trouble. 14 b3 was a better move, stopping Black's knight from coming to c4.

14...♘c4

Threatening both the b2- and e4-pawns. The following 'combinative defence' simply does not work.

15 ♗d4 ♗xe4 16 ♗xg7 ♗xf3 17 ♕xf3 ♔xg7 18 ♕g4+ ♔h8 19 ♗xa8 f5!

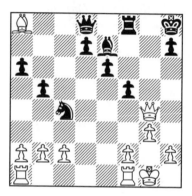

A highly effective zwischenzug. 19...♕xa8 20 ♕d4+ f6 21 ♕xd7 is less convincing.

20 ♕d4+ ♗f6 21 ♕a7 ♕xa8 22 ♕xd7 ♘e5 0-1

After 23 ♕xe6 ♘f3+ 24 ♔h1 ♘g5+ White loses his queen.

Taking this idea one step further, a player should also focus on winning even if he only needs a draw. In his influential book on chess psychology Nicolai Krogius related the story about how he learned to focus on winning when a draw would have been enough for title norms. Needless to say this is very difficult to do, but this kind of courage pays huge dividends in terms of what someone can achieve.

Here are the two games from Krogius's story, the first having been played before his revelation and the second afterwards:

Game 20
N.Krogius-V.Tarasov
USSR Championship,
Leningrad 1949
King's Indian Defence

---

1 d4 ♘f6 2 c4 d6 3 ♘f3 g6

The King's Indian is the perfect choice against a player who needs a draw. There is no easy way of simplifying the game, which almost guarantees a full blooded struggle.

4 g3 ♗g7 5 ♗g2 0-0 6 0-0 ♘bd7 7 ♘c3 e5 8 e4 exd4 9 ♘xd4 ♖e8 10 h3 ♘c5 11 ♖e1 a5

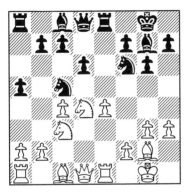

12 ♗f4

Having played such positions many

times as White I'd probably choose 12 b3 myself, and after 12...♘fd7 13 ♗e3 ♘e5 14 ♕c2 ♘ed3 15 ♖ed1 White is able to repel boarders.

12...♘fd7 13 ♗e3 c6 14 ♕e2

White feels the need to defend the c4-pawn but the queen isn't that well placed when opposite the rook on e8.

14...a4 15 ♖ad1 ♕a5 16 ♕c2 ♘e5 17 ♘b1?

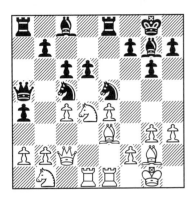

This passive move is a sign of a very negative frame of mind and it should just lose a pawn. White has to play 17 b3, when 17...♕b4 18 ♖e2 holds the position together.

17...♕b4?

Missing 17...♘ed3 18 ♖e2 ♘b4, picking up the pawn on a2.

18 b3 axb3 19 axb3 f5!?

Black continues his bullying tactics.

20 exf5 ♘ed3 21 ♖f1 ♗xd4!?

A non-stereotypical decision, giving up his King's Indian bishop on g7 in return for generating concrete threats. But what is especially interesting about this is that White would have got quite a good position had he be thinking in more ambitious terms.

22 ♗xd4 ♗xf5

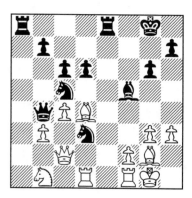

23 g4

23 ♗c3! is actually quite good for White, as after 23...♕xb3 24 ♕xb3 ♘xb3 he wins a piece with 25 g4.

23...♘e1 24 ♕c3 ♕xc3 25 ♗xc3

And here 25 ♘xc3 would have been stronger: for example, 25...♘xg2 26 gxf5 ♘f4 27 ♗e3 attacking f4 and d6.

After Krogius's move Black is simply better.

25...♘xg2 26 gxf5 ♘f4 27 fxg6 hxg6 28 ♖xd6?

A blunder. White would still be on the board after 28 ♗d2 but this was evidently not Krogius's day.

28...♘e4 29 ♗b4 ♘xd6 30 ♗xd6 ♘xh3+ 31 ♔h2 ♘g5 32 ♘c3 ♘e4 33 ♘xe4 ♖xe4 34 ♗c5 ♖d8 35 ♗e3 ♖d3 36 ♖b1 ♖e8 37 b4 ♖e4 38 c5 ♔f7 39 b5 ♔e6 40 bxc6 bxc6

Black is making heavy weather of this endgame but he gets there in the end.

41 ♖b8 ♔d5 42 ♖g8 ♖e6 43 ♔g2 ♔e4 44 ♔f1 ♖xe3 45 fxe3 ♔xe3 46 ♖d8 ♔f4 47 ♖d4+ ♔f5 48 ♔f2 ♖e5 49 ♖c4 ♔e6 0-1

> ## Game 21
> ### N.Krogius-F.Gheorghiu
> Sochi 1964
> *Sicilian Defence*

1 e4 c5 2 ♘f3 d6 3 d4

The fact that White is playing an Open Sicilian (3 d4) rather than a solid line such as 3 ♗b5+ should have tipped Gheorghiu off to the fact that his opponent might not be making a special attempt to play for a draw. Had he heeded these early signs he might have played less riskily later on.

3...cxd4 4 ♘xd4 ♘f6 5 ♘c3 a6 6 ♗e2 e6 7 0-0 ♕c7 8 f4 ♗e7 9 ♕e1 ♘c6 10 ♗e3 ♗d7 11 ♕g3 g6 12 ♔h1

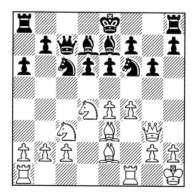

12...h5?!

I don't believe Black would have played this way had he not believed that White was over a barrel. The kingside should normally be where Black's king resides, but that is not going to happen after an advance of the h-pawn.

13 ♕e1 h4 14 ♗f3 ♘h5 15 ♘de2 ♘a5

16 ♗d4 ♖h7 17 b3 ♘c6 18 ♗f2

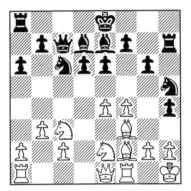

18...♘g3+

An unsound pawn sacrifice, no doubt prompted by the same 'draw in the hand' mentality as 12...h5. Unfortunately for Black there is no compensation and Krogius meanwhile is staying as cool as a cucumber.

19 ♘xg3 hxg3 20 ♗xg3 g5 21 e5!

This powerful move cuts right across Black's attempts to get the e5-square for his knight. Now his king will become a real problem.

21...gxf4 22 exd6! ♗xd6

On 22...♕xd6 White can play 23 ♖d1 after which 23...fxg3 24 ♖xd6 ♖xh2+ 25 ♔g1 ♗xd6 26 ♘e4 ♗e5 27 ♘xg3 ♖h7 28 c3 leaves Black with inadequate com-

pensation for the queen. Admittedly this might have been better than the game.

23 ♘d5 0-0-0

The dubious point.

24 ♘xc7 fxg3 25 h3 ♗xc7 26 ♖d1 ♖dh8

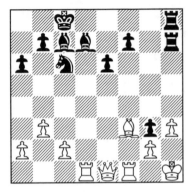

27 ♖xd7!

This exchange sacrifice puts the issue beyond doubt. In addition to enjoying a material advantage White is now on the attack.

27...♔xd7 28 ♗xc6+ ♔xc6 29 ♕e4+ ♔b6 30 ♕d4+ ♔c6 31 ♖f3 b5 32 ♕a7 ♖xh3+

Desperation.

33 gxh3 ♖xh3+ 34 ♔g2 ♖h2+ 35 ♔f1 ♖h1+ 36 ♔e2 ♖h2+ 37 ♔d3 g2 38 ♖xf7 ♗b6 39 ♕b7+ ♔c5 40 b4+ 1-0

17) Master the art of deception

Deception tends not to be discussed too much in the West despite the fact that it is extremely common in chess, other games and indeed the natural world. Perhaps the reason for this is that it sounds somewhat underhand, yet deception is an essential skill.

The first step towards mastering deception is to understand the different forms it can take. Mindful of such possibilities it's then easier to put flesh on the bones by identifying examples of deception when it occurs. Here are the most common forms:

Luring

One of the best known lures is to offer a 'poisoned pawn', a pawn sacrifice which is highly dangerous to accept. The problem is that your opponent will usually look at such a pawn with great suspicion, so your best chance of acceptance is to make it look as if it could be a blunder.

Away from the actual board there are some cases of players attempting to dope an opponent before the game, for example with offers of alcohol, though famously this once backfired. Before playing Stahlberg in one game, Najdorf kindly invited his Swedish colleague to lunch and promptly started plying him with alcohol. Stahlberg was very fond of the stuff so he could not bring himself to refuse. But as the lunch progressed it got to the point where even Mrs Najdorf whispered to her husband about how unfair this was. Najdorf whispered back that Stahlberg was a grown man and could make his own decisions.

The time came for the game and Stahlberg was completely drunk. But he proceeded to play one good move after another until Najdorf's position was quite lost. Suddenly, with victory close at hand, Stahlberg offered a draw which Najdorf had little choice but to accept.

After the game a spectator asked the wobbly Stahlberg why he had offered a draw in such a good position. "How could I beat the man who had just bought me such an excellent lunch?"

Another example of a lure is to present the possibility of a draw in front of someone by taking an opportunity to repeat a position a couple of times. This gets them to use time on the clock searching for a way to avoid it whilst luring them into a false sense of security by making it look as if you are happy with a draw. The first time I played Tony Miles he did this against me and I quickly went along with it for a threefold repetition and a draw. After the game he told me that this was one of his favourite ploys; had I used too much time on the clock he would have varied on his third move and kept playing.

Goading

Goading is essentially a stronger form of the lure. Examples include 'playing dead' by running yourself desperately short of thinking time. Occasionally a player will attempt to anger his opponent in order to get him to lose his cool and objectivity. Usually this involves means which are blatantly against the rules, but enforcing these rules can be a tricky business. One of the most famous examples of a goad was when Tony Miles played 1 e4 a6 against Anatoly Karpov in Skara, 1980. It seems that Karpov lost his cool, played in an uncharacteristically aggressive style and lost.

Bluffing

In a sense this is the opposite of the lure in that you want to feign strength rather than weakness in order to provoke concessions. There's often an element of bluff in the game of confident and aggressive attackers. For example, both Mikhail Tal and Garry Kasparov have been accused of bluffing.

Mimicry

Some players feign friendship before and even during the game in order to put their opponents off their guard. The US Grandmaster John Fedorowicz once told me a nice story about how he played in a tournament with former World Champion Tigran Petrosian. He couldn't figure out why Petrosian was always smiling and being unexpectedly friendly towards him until the light finally dawned: they were due to play in the last round and Petrosian thought it wise to be on good terms in case he should need a quick draw.

Other forms of mimicry include playing your opponent's own moves (usually his openings) against him so that he faces the problem of playing against himself. This technique was in fact used by David Bronstein in his 1951 World Championship match against Botvinnik.

Decoy

A good example of the decoy in chess is a strategy by which you attack on one side of the board in order to tie your opponent's pieces down to defence and then switch to the point at which he's least well defended.

Change in Tempo

This is a very common tactic; you get your opponent acclimatized to a slow game and then angle for a breakthrough so that the game changes pace.

There are more sophisticated ways of imbuing your entire game with a deceptive element, for example by playing multipurpose moves wherever possible. These will cause your opponent to misconstrue your real intentions or at least divide his forces.

Another example is that if you've been successful with a particular opening variation, be wary of repeating it for too long. The problem is that you become quite predictable by doing so and some cunning opponents may be well prepared.

One of the best examples of deception was Bobby Fischer's switch to the English Opening (1 c4) in his 1972 match against Boris Spassky. With Fischer having previously stated that 1 e4 is "best by test", this must have come as a real shock to Spassky who found himself totally wrong-footed by a newly unpredictable opponent. This tactic has been repeated by leading players on many occasions since.

> **Game 22**
> **R.Fischer-B.Spassky**
> World Championship
> (6th game), Reykjavik 1972
> Queen's Gambit Declined

1 c4!

A psychological masterstroke by Fischer, and this game destroyed the idea that he was a one-trick pony. Although Spassky was very well prepared against Fischer's known repertoire with 1 e4, he found himself less able to deal with the American's unknown repertoire.

1...e6 2 ♘f3 d5 3 d4

Transposing to the Queen's Gambit Declined.

3...♘f6 4 ♘c3 ♗e7 5 ♗g5 0-0 6 e3 h6 7 ♗h4 b6

Spassky chooses the most dependable weapon in his armoury, but this could hardly have come as a surprise.

8 cxd5 ♘xd5 9 ♗xe7 ♕xe7 10 ♘xd5

exd5 11 ♖c1 ♗e6 12 ♕a4 c5 13 ♕a3 ♖c8 14 ♗b5!?

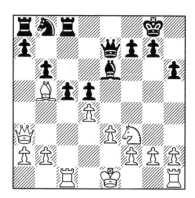

Making it difficult for Black to develop his queen's knight whilst provoking a further weakening of Black's pawns. This move had in fact been played two years earlier and against Efim Geller, one of Spassky's seconds. But needless to say this would not have been a main topic for the Russians' studies.

14...a6

The following year it was Geller who improved on Black's play with

14...♕b7!. J.Timman-E.Geller, Hilversum 1973, continued 15 dxc5 bxc5 16 ♖xc5 ♖xc5 17 ♕xc5 ♘a6! 18 ♗xa6 (18 ♕c6 ♕xc6 19 ♗xc6 ♖b8! would allow Black to recover his pawn with a good game, 20 b3 being bad because of 20...♖c8 21 ♘d4 ♘b4 etc) 18...♗xa6 19 ♕a3 ♕c4 20 ♔d2? (20 ♕c3 is the best try but again Black is better after 20...♖b8 21 ♕xc4 dxc4 22 b3! cxb3 23 axb3 ♖xb3) 20...♕g4 21 ♖g1 d4! 22 ♘xd4 ♕h4 23 ♖e1 ♕xf2+ and White's exposed king cost him the game.

15 dxc5 bxc5 16 0-0

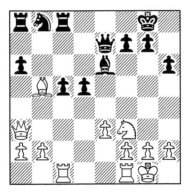

16...♖a7?!

Another improvement for Black subsequently emerged in the game S.Makarichev-Z.Sturua, Moscow 1979. Black played 16...♕a7!? and after 17 ♗a4 a5 18 ♕d3 ♘d7 19 ♗xd7 ♕xd7 20 ♖fd1 ♖ab8 the position was about equal.

17 ♗e2 ♘d7

The precedent for 14 ♗b5 was S.Furman-E.Geller, Moscow 1970, which went 17...a5 18 ♖c3! ♘d7 19 ♖fc1 ♖e8?! 20 ♗b5 ♗g4!? and now 21 ♖xc5! ♘xc5 22 ♗xe8 ♕xe8 23 ♕xc5 ♖b7 24 b3

would have won a pawn. Spassky's move may be a slight improvement but in any case White stands better.

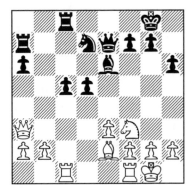

18 ♘d4! ♕f8?

Fischer's reply opens the position up for his bishop. Black should have tried 18...♘f6 when 19 ♘b3 c4 20 ♕xe7 ♖xe7 21 ♘d4 might be tenable for Black.

19 ♘xe6 fxe6 20 e4! d4

Or if 20...♘f6 there would follow 21 exd5 exd5 22 b3 when Black's 'hanging pawn' duo on c5 and d5 would prove a nightmare to defend.

21 f4 ♕e7 22 e5!

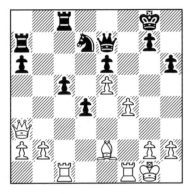

Black's main problem here is in

finding a decent square for his knight, especially after this powerful move. One of the points is that 22...♘b6 can be answered by 23 ♖fd1 when 23...♘d5 24 ♖xd4 loses a pawn for Black.

22...♖b8 23 ♗c4! ♔h8

After 23...♘b6 24 ♕b3 the knight is pinned against the rook on b8.

24 ♕h3 ♘f8 25 b3 a5 26 f5!

Switching to a direct attack on Black's king. Fischer finishes the game in his usual majestic style.

26...exf5 27 ♖xf5 ♘h7 28 ♖cf1 ♕d8 29 ♕g3 ♖e7 30 h4

Taking g5 away from Black's knight.

30...♖bb7 31 e6 ♖bc7 32 ♕e5 ♕e8 33 a4! ♕d8 34 ♖1f2 ♕e8 35 ♖2f3 ♕d8 36 ♗d3 ♕e8 37 ♕e4!

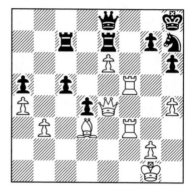

Threatening mate via 38 ♖f8+.

37...♘f6 38 ♖xf6! gxf6 39 ♖xf6 ♔g8 40 ♗c4 ♔h8 41 ♕f4 1-0

18) Know your weapons well

"You should not have a favourite weapon. To become over-familiar with one weapon is as much a fault as not knowing it sufficiently well. You should not copy others, but use weapons which you can handle properly. It is bad for commanders and troopers to have likes and dislikes. These are things you must learn thoroughly."

Myamoto Musashi (*The Book of Five Rings*)

I have often seen it advised that a player should have pet openings that he knows better than his opponents, and at first sight this seems to be excellent advice. Yet I myself tend towards Musashi's view that one should be more of an all-rounder. The reason for this is that players who experience a broad sweep of chess ideas tend to develop their game as a whole far more effectively than those who specialize in one little cranny.

Looking for examples of overspecialization I would point to players such as Lev Polugaevsky and Lev Alburt. I've heard it said that Polugaevsky never quite scaled the heights because he never played the Ruy Lopez whilst Alburt fished in even narrower streams.

On the other hand every single World Champion from Wilhelm Steinitz to Viswanathan Anand has had broad experience of main line openings, something which in my view is far from accidental. Not only does such wholesome food provide appropriate sustenance to a growing player, such openings will be reliable weapons in critical tournament situations.

In the following game it seems as if Black was short of a particularly good defence against 1 d4, as after he played the reliable Slav Defence it became clear that he did not know it properly and was lost after just a few moves.

Game 23
S.Gordon-D.Robertson
European Union
Championship, Liverpool 2008
Slav Defence

---

1 d4 d5 2 c4 c6 3 ♘f3 ♘f6 4 ♘c3 ♗f5?
This is known to be a mistake here.

Black's main options are 4...dxc4 (a regular Slav Defence); 4...e6 (a Semi-Slav); and the trendy 4...a6.

5 cxd5 cxd5?

And here Black should play 5...♘xd5. Now he gets into trouble.

6 ♕b3 e6?

Already a losing move because Black gets zero compensation for the pawn on b7.

The only option here is the grim 6...♗c8!, but this is not an easy move to play and in any case Black's position would be difficult.

problems in this position.

14 ♕xb6 ♘xb6 15 ♘e5 ♖fc8 16 ♖fc1 ♘e8 17 ♘c6 ♗f8 18 ♘bxa7

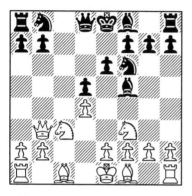

7 ♕xb7 ♘bd7 8 e3 ♗d6 9 ♗e2 0-0 10 ♕a6 ♕b8 11 0-0 h6 12 ♘b5 ♗e7 13 ♗d2 ♕b6

The very fact that Black feels obliged to trade queens into a pawn-down endgame is a testimony to his

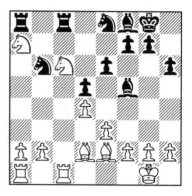

With the second pawn falling Black's game is hopeless. He fights on gamely but could have saved himself the rest.

18...♖c7 19 ♘b5 ♖cc8 20 b3 ♘d6 21 a4 ♘dc4 22 bxc4 ♖xc6 23 c5 e5? 24 cxb6 1-0

19) Empty the mind

"The mind must always be in the state of 'flowing', for when it stops anywhere that means that the flow is interrupted and it is this interruption that is injurious to the well-being of the mind. In the case of the swordsman, it means death.

"When the swordsman stands against his opponent, he is not to think of the opponent, nor of himself, nor of his enemy's sword movements. He just stands there with his sword which, forgetful of all technique, is ready only to follow the dictates of the unconscious. The man has effaced himself as the wielder of the sword. When he strikes, it is not the man but the sword in the hand of the unconscious that strikes."

Takuan Soho

The Soviet World Champion Mikhail Botvinnik was famous for his excellent preparation, setting the standard for future generations. One of Botvinnik's tenets was to do nothing on the morning of a game so as to keep a clear head. This seems similar to the state of 'mushin' (no mind) which is regarded by martial artists as the ideal mental state for combat.

In my own chess experience I've found that a clear head is a distinct advantage. Essentially I try to follow Botvinnik's advice about doing nothing before a game, though I will occasionally read a book.

Why does it work? A simple explanation is that if the mind is freed of distractions there will be more processing power available for the chess. It may also be much deeper than this, for example a *mushin* state may enable people to tap into the subconscious mind and play more intuitively. The most immediately relevant point is that having a clear head helps the cause of victory.

What strategies should someone follow for trying to ensure this? Something that I've found works well for me is to regard my only job in a game as being to play one good move after another and let everything else (for example rating, norms and prizes) take care of itself. Obviously it's not ideal to play after a hard day's work and many players would do well to consider alternatives, for example restricting themselves to weekend events. If this is not possible then try to take a break between finishing work and playing the game, and either use this to meditate or listen to some relaxing music.

I learned by experience about the benefits of having a clear head. At one time I used to prepare too much in the morning before a game but I gradually moved towards preparing very little or even not at all. One of my best tournament results was to win the Gausdal International in 1997 but in this tournament I did not prepare at all, at least not in a chess sense. Before each game I went for a long walk in the Norwegian mountains, just enjoying the beautiful surroundings and the peace and quiet. I arrived at each game in a wonderful frame of mind and found myself playing with unusual ease and cheer.

Here is one of my games from this tournament.

Game 24
N.Davies-T.Thorhallsson
Arnold Cup, Gausdal 1997
Réti Opening

---

1 ♘f3 d5 2 c4 e6 3 g3 ♘f6 4 ♗g2 ♗e7 5 0-0 0-0 6 b3

An invitation to play a chess game without the usual issue of theory.

6 d4 would transpose into a Catalan in which the temptation to study before the game would be much greater. I had also noticed that my opponent played very well when the ball came directly onto the bat but was less comfortable with slow positional manoeuvring.

6...c5 7 e3 ♘c6 8 ♕e2 b6 9 ♗b2 ♗b7 10 ♖d1 ♖c8 11 d3 ♕c7 12 ♘c3

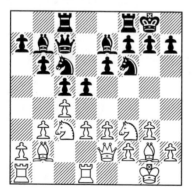

12...♖cd8

My opponent was not looking too

comfortable and this is a dubious-looking move. The natural 12...♖fd8 should be better.

13 ♖ac1 ♕b8 14 cxd5 ♘xd5

On 14...exd5 White plays 15 d4 followed by 16 dxc5, when Black has to accept either an isolated d-pawn (by recapturing on c5 with a piece) or 'hanging pawns' on d5 and c5.

15 ♘xd5 ♖xd5

Here too 15...exd5 would be answered by 16 d4, when Black would get some pawn weaknesses.

After the capture with the rook on d5 there are no pawn weaknesses to target so I had to proceed in a more tactical vein. And it's here that having a clear head is especially useful.

16 d4 cxd4 17 ♘xd4 ♘xd4 18 exd4

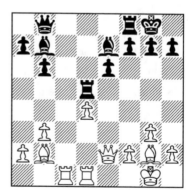

18...♖a5!

The best square for the rook.

On 18...♖f5 I wanted to play 19 d5.

For example, 19...♗c5 20 ♖xc5 bxc5 21 ♕g4 f6 (or 21...g6 22 ♗e4 ♗xd5 23 ♗xf5 exf5 24 ♕h4 etc) 22 dxe6 and here a sample line runs 22...♖g5 23 ♕c4 ♔h8 24 e7 ♖e8 25 ♕b5 ♖xe7 (25...♗xg2 26 ♕xb8 ♖xb8 27 ♖d8+ wins) 26 ♗xb7 ♖xb7 27 ♕xb7 ♕xb7 28 ♖d8 mate.

19 d5 ♖xa2 20 dxe6 ♗xg2 21 ♔xg2 ♕b7+?

Losing. 21...♗f6! was mandatory and 22 exf7+ ♔h8 23 ♖c2 ♖xb2 24 ♖xb2 ♗xb2 25 ♕xb2 ♕b7+ 26 ♔g1 ♕xf7 is drawish.

22 ♔g1 ♗f6 23 ♖d7!

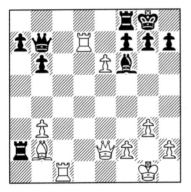

Winning.

23...♕a8

Or if 23...♖xb2 White can play 24 exf7+ ♖xf7 (24...♔h8 25 ♕e8 ♕a8 26 ♕xa8 ♖xa8 27 ♖e1 and 28 ♖e8+ wins) 25 ♕e8+ ♖f8 26 ♕e6+ winning the queen.

24 exf7+ ♔h8

After 24...♖xf7 there follows 25 ♕e6 ♕f8 26 ♖xf7 ♕xf7 27 ♖c8+ etc.

25 ♖e1 ♖xb2 26 ♕e8! ♖b1! 27 ♕xf8+ ♕xf8 28 ♖xb1

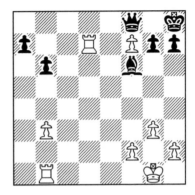

Despite the fact that my rook has been distracted from e1, there is still time to bring it back. The threat is 29 ♖e1 and 30 ♖e8.

28...♗c3

The main variation I had calculated was 28...♕c5 29 ♖e1 h5 (or 29...h6 30 ♖e8+ ♔h7 31 f8♘+ ♔g8 32 ♘e6+ winning the queen) 30 ♖e8+ ♔h7 31 f8♕ ♕c1+ 32 ♔g2 ♕c6+ 33 f3 ♕xd7 34 ♕g8+ ♔h6 35 ♕e6 etc.

29 ♖bd1 g6 30 ♖d8 ♗b4 31 ♖xf8+ ♗xf8 32 ♖d7 a5 33 ♖b7 ♔g7 34 ♖xb6 ♔xf7 35 ♖b7+ ♔g8 1-0

20) Walk, but never talk

During my teenage years I was a great admirer of Mikhail Botvinnik and read about how he liked to arrive early to the game and stay seated for most of it. Other players often arrive late and then get up between moves to talk to their friends. Which is the better model to follow?

There's little doubt in my mind that to be able to concentrate well players should tend towards Botvinnik's approach and attempt to cultivate this if it does not come naturally. Having said that it helps to have an occasional walk between moves and David Bronstein once advised me to take a 20 minute walk before the game. I have my own version of this which is to let tension dissolve from the shoulders by allowing the arms to swing naturally. There's a case for taking this even further by learning some physical and mental relaxation techniques that can be found in disciplines such as yoga, chi kung, autogenics or meditation. I have used both autogenic and chi kung techniques and found them very useful.

Talking during a game is another matter altogether. First of all it is against the rules (this prevents players discussing their games) and secondly it is one of the most destructive things someone can do to their concentration. I see this as being akin to taking a phone call during the working day – it can take a while to refocus. So I make it a rule not to talk during my games.

Botvinnik's habit of arriving early is also a good one to follow as it allows a player to settle in and write the players' names at the top of the score sheet prior to the game beginning. Many players make a habit of arriving late, perhaps because they want to show that they can sacrifice time on the clock and still win or present their egos with an 'excuse' ("I arrived late and ran into time trouble") should they lose. Needless to say a late arrival does not optimize a player's chances so they should tend towards Botvinnik's approach.

Here's a game in which time-trouble played a part.

Game 25
A.Karpov-H.Mecking
Hastings 1971/72
Sicilian Defence

---

1 e4 c5 2 ♘f3 d6 3 d4 cxd4 4 ♘xd4 ♘f6

5 ♘c3 a6 6 ♗e2 e5 7 ♘b3 ♗e6 8 f4 ♕c7 9 a4 ♘c6 10 f5 ♗xb3 11 cxb3 ♕b6 12 ♗g5 ♗e7 13 ♗xf6 ♗xf6 14 ♘d5 ♕a5+ 15 ♕d2 ♕xd2+ 16 ♔xd2 ♗g5+ 17 ♔d3 0-0 18 h4 ♗d8 19 ♖ac1 a5 20 ♔d2 ♖b8 21 g4 ♘b4 22 ♗c4 ♘xd5 23 ♗xd5 g5 24 fxg6 hxg6 25 ♔d3 ♔g7

White has a clear advantage here

because of his better-placed pieces. But it looks as if there will be a long hard struggle ahead until Mecking caves in during his habitual time trouble.

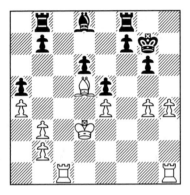

26 h5 ♗b6?!

Already wrong. 26...gxh5! was a much better defence: for example, 27 ♖xh5 (27 gxh5 ♔h6 28 ♖cf1 b5 is not bad either) 27...♔g6 intending 28...b5 looks quite tenable.

27 ♖h3 ♗c5?!

27...gxh5 is still the right idea.

28 ♖f1

Threatening 29 h6+ and suddenly putting Black in trouble. 28...gxh5 is not so good anymore because of 29 gxh5 ♔h6 30 ♖f6+ etc.

28...f6 29 hxg6 ♔xg6 30 ♖fh1 ♖be8

It's also too late for 30...b5: for example, 31 axb5 ♖xb5 32 ♖h6+ ♔g5 33 ♔e2 starts weaving a mating net around Black's king.

31 ♖h7 ♔g5 32 ♔e2

White could have forced matters with 32 ♗f7, but instead just calmly improves his position. This can be particularly unpleasant for a player who is short of time, whereas meeting direct

threats is relatively easy.

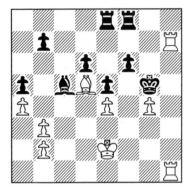

32...♔f4

After 32...♔g6 White wins with 33 ♖1h6+ ♔g5 34 ♔f3 b6 35 ♖h5+ ♔g6 36 ♗c6 ♖d8 37 ♗d7 threatening 38 ♗f5+.

33 ♖1h3 ♗d4

Or 33...♔xg4 34 ♖h1 ♖g8 35 ♖7h4+ ♔g5 36 ♔f3 (threatening 37 ♖g4 mate) 36...f5 37 ♖h5+ ♔f6 38 ♖xf5+ etc.

34 ♖g7 1-0

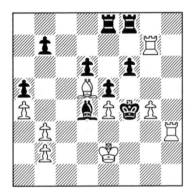

The threat of ♖f3 mate is unavoidable.

One of the great things about playing chess is that not much equipment is required. For many US tournaments the players need to bring their own set, board and clock but generally speaking these are provided. The only essential equipment is a pen with which to write down the moves. Some of us like to take a spare in case one of them runs out.

Ear plugs are another useful piece of equipment, especially for those who are sensitive to noise. Amongst Grandmasters, I know that Anatoly Vaiser and myself use them, but with variable playing conditions more should consider it. The deaf World Champion Tigran Petrosian had quite an advantage in that he could simply turn off his hearing aid if the noise level rose too high. This may in fact have been the decisive factor in his 1971 Candidates Match with Robert Hübner in which the sensitive German Grandmaster was badly affected by the noisy venue.

In the Gausdal Chess Festival of 1993, a number of bleary-eyed players came to breakfast complaining about the noise of building work which commenced at 7am. They had tried unsuccessfully to complain to the hotel management; I slept just fine because I had brought my ear plugs with me. Ear plugs also helped me to win my game against the Russian Grandmaster Yuri Razuvaev when I failed to hear his draw offer and he blundered on his next move. I thought he said something but I really was not sure. Had I heard him offer the draw, I might well have accepted as the position was fairly level at the time. After that I went

on to register a Grandmaster title qualifying score and ascended to Grandmaster status later that year.

<hr>

Game 26
N.Davies-Y.Razuvaev
Gausdal 1993
Sicilian Defence

<hr>

1 e4

My preparation for this game consisted of asking Einar Gausel what he thought about Yuri Razuvaev's play. "Go for his king" was the answer, "he really doesn't like it". So I resolved to open with 1 e4 and make it up as I went along.

1...c5

With so many games on the databases featuring my playing 2 d3, the Sicilian became a popular choice against me. In reply I chose a line that featured more heavily at the Bolton Quickplay than the Soviet Championship.

2 ♘c3 ♘c6 3 ♗b5!? ♘d4 4 ♘f3 e6 5 0-0 ♘e7 6 ♘xd4 cxd4 7 ♘e2 a6 8 ♗d3

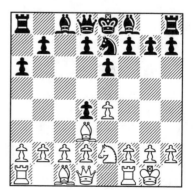

8 ♗a4 has also been played here but following Gausel's advice I wanted to point the bishop at my opponent's kingside.

8...♘c6 9 c3 dxc3

They do not usually play this way but maybe they should.

In practice 9...♗c5 has been a far more popular reply but then 10 b4 ♗a7 11 cxd4 ♘xd4?! (11...0-0 is a much better move) 12 ♗b2 ♕f6 13 ♔h1 g5 14 ♖c1 d6 15 f4 gave White a strong initiative in V.Baklan-A.Cherniaev, European Championship, Istanbul 2003.

10 dxc3 ♗e7 11 ♗c2 0-0 12 ♕d3

Lining one's queen and bishop up against h7 is not the most sophisticated way to play chess but I was starting to sense that Mr Gausel was absolutely right. My opponent seemed uncomfortable.

12...♘e5?!

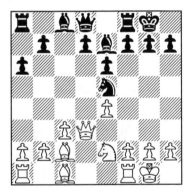

I don't particularly like this move here because the knight will get kicked around. I think my opponent played this way because of the Gausel diagnosis; Razuvaev does not like having his king threatened.

Just 12...d6 looks better to me, intending to meet 13 e5 with 13...g6.

13 ♕h3 f6 14 ♘d4

Making room for the f-pawn's advance.

14...♕c7 15 f4 ♘c6

After the game Razuvaev felt that 15...♘f7 would have been better, keeping the knight in the vicinity of his king. After having played 12 ...♘e5 this certainly makes sense, though whether he should have played that at all is a moot point.

16 ♗e3 ♗c5 17 ♖ad1 ♘xd4 18 ♗xd4 b5 19 f5 ♗xd4+ 20 ♖xd4

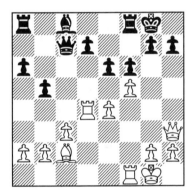

In spite of White's primitive-looking play Black is in some trouble here. Because of the pressure against the pawn on e6 he cannot develop the bishop on c8. And meanwhile White is getting ready to take pot shots at Black's king.

20...♕e5 21 ♗b3 a5?!

After this White's initiative nets a pawn.

Black should have removed his king from the a2-g8 diagonal with 21...♔h8, though this is still far from pleasant for

Black after 22 ♖f3 ♖a7 23 ♕g4 intending 24 ♖h3.

22 fxe6 dxe6 23 ♖f5! ♕c7 24 ♖h5

Hitting both the h7- and e6-pawns, with the one on b5 as a back up. At least one of them must fall.

24...g5 25 ♗xe6+ ♗xe6 26 ♕xe6+ ♖f7

It might have been better to exchange queens with 26...♕f7 27 ♕xf7+ ♖xf7, but then 28 h4 will be winning for White.

27 e5! ♖d8 28 exf6 ♔f8

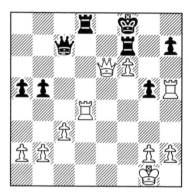

29 ♕e5

A crowd had gathered around my board by this stage, including several of the hotel staff, and it seems that all of them had seen 29 ♕xf7+! which wins on the spot. Fortunately my move also wins.

29...♖xd4 30 cxd4 ♕c1+ 31 ♔f2 ♖c7 32 ♔g3 1-0

With my king safe it's all over.

Recently I acquired some ear defenders of the type used by the ground staff at airports. These tend to be somewhat obtrusive for use at large tournaments, but for noisy club nights they can be very helpful if a player is willing to put up with some teasing from their peers.

A relatively new issue is that of the mobile phone, with the current legislation calling for players whose phones ring to lose by default. Arbiters generally advise players to turn their phones off at the start of a game, but some of them now turn themselves on again and beep to announce that the battery is running low. At the time of writing such beeps appear to be a grey area, but the safest advice seems to be to remove the battery from your phone prior to the start of play.

Chapter Three

The Opening

"To visualise the beginning of this evolution we may surmise that at an ancient date, when players of original talent, whom today we would call 'natural' players, predominated over all others, some unknown genius, with a penchant for collecting information, made notes of the beginnings of good games, compiled them, classified them and exhibited his work to a few friends. As a natural consequence, some of the more industrious and intelligent learners would, in the first dozen moves, overcome superior players of that day, by employing the tactical manoeuvres gleaned from the manuscript of their compiler friend. One can imagine the surprise of spectators and the wrath of the defeated masters as the observed newcomers, without natural talent, waging a strong fight purely with the aid of a book of compiled information."

Emanuel Lasker (*Lasker's Manual of Chess*)

There is a huge amount of literature devoted to chess openings yet despite this it remains one of the most misunderstood aspects of the game. Many players believe that they need to memorize countless variations before they play a match or tournament, but this is far from being the case. A knowledge of principles and ideas is far more important, especially at amateur level. Indeed, my extensive experience of working with students has shown that very few club games follow 'theory' for more than a few moves at which point memorization becomes useless.

With the rules in this section I hope to supply some much needed perspective on this thorny problem of the opening.

21) Aim to reach a playable middlegame

The importance of the opening tends to be overestimated, especially at club level. To some extent it might be argued that this is because so many books and DVDs are available on this stage of the game, but that does not explain why a market for these products is there in the first place. It seems reasonable to think that this market has been driven by the fact that opening knowledge presents a convenient way to rationalize losses ("I didn't know the opening") without the need to blame overall skill.

Having analysed hundreds of club players' games I've come to believe that 'openings knowledge' as such is rarely responsible for either victory or defeat, not least because the games rarely follow recognizable 'theory' for more than 5-10 moves. It certainly helps if someone knows the kind of thing they should be doing in a certain type of position, but this is a far cry from knowing an extensive number of detailed opening variations.

This argues heavily in favour of players at club level using simple, commonsense openings from which they know how to handle the middlegame, and indeed this is how Portisch himself and many other top Grandmasters started their careers. There will be time enough to sharpen these weapons when a player becomes a full-time professional. And many players, such as Britain's Michael Adams, choose to adopt a commonsense approach even then.

The following game was played by Portisch early in his career and features a nice win using the Closed Sicilian. Later in his career he became known as one of the greatest connoisseurs of the opening, so his choice here deserves attention.

Game 27
L.Portisch-G.Barcza
Hungarian Championship,
Budapest 1961
Sicilian Defence

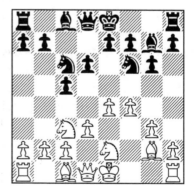

1 e4 c5 2 ♘c3 ♘c6 3 g3 g6 4 ♗g2 ♗g7 5 d3 d6 6 f4 ♘f6 7 ♘ge2!?

An interesting twist because usually the knight goes to f3. Portisch's idea is

---

that he can later bring this knight to g3 from where it helps to support a king-side attack.

7...♗d7 8 h3 ♖b8 9 g4 ♘d4

One of the points of White's play is that after 9...b5 10 ♘g3 b4 his knight on c3 will drop back to e2, this square having been cleared in the nick of time. Note that this is why White played 8 h3 rather than 8 0-0; he wanted to free the e2-square before Black got in ...b7-b5-b4.

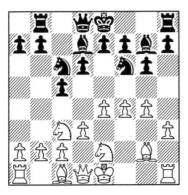

10 ♘g3 ♗c6 11 0-0 0-0 12 ♗e3 ♘d7 13 ♕d2 e6 14 ♘d1

This regrouping manoeuvre is typical strategy in the Closed Sicilian: White prepares to drive Black's knight away from the d4-square with the advance 15 c3.

14...d5 15 c3 ♘b5 16 a4 ♘c7 17 f5 dxe4 18 ♘xe4 ♗xe4

Exchanging off White's well-placed knight but giving up the bishop pair. The cold-blooded 18...exf5 19 gxf5 ♘d5 might have been better, though I can understand why Black might have some concerns for his king after 20 ♗h6.

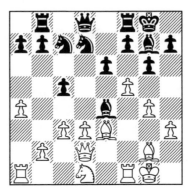

19 ♗xe4 exf5 20 gxf5 ♕h4 21 ♕g2 ♗h6 22 ♗f2

Calmly driving Black's queen back. 22 ♗xb7 would be risky because of the weakness of White's king and Black's piece activity.

22...♕d8 23 ♘e3

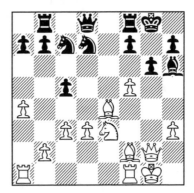

23...♘f6

Black quite rightly senses the danger to his king and rushes reserves over to defend himself. After a solid-looking move like 23...b6 White can play 24 fxg6 hxg6 25 ♘f5!, for example 25...♗g7 26 ♗h4 ♗f6 27 ♘h6+ ♔h8 28 ♖xf6! ♘xf6 29 ♖f1 etc.

24 ♘g4 ♘xg4 25 ♕xg4 ♘d5

Giving up the c5-pawn. 25...b6 would be answered by 26 ♗h4 ♕d7 27 ♔h1 threatening 28 fxg6 ♕xg4 (not check) 29 gxh7+.

26 ♕f3 ♘f6 27 ♗xc5 ♘xe4 28 dxe4

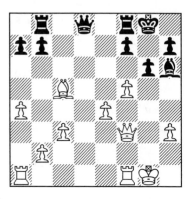

28...♖e8?!

Losing immediately. Black could have struggled on by giving up the exchange.

29 fxg6 ♕g5+ 30 ♔h1 ♕xg6 31 ♖g1 ♗g5

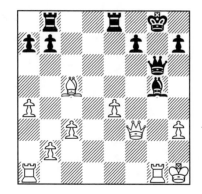

32 ♖xg5! 1-0

After 32...♕xg5 33 ♖g1 Black loses his queen.

22) Play your own game

"The individual is of first importance, not the system. Remember that man created method and not that method created man, and do not strain yourself into someone's pre-conceived patter, which unquestioningly would be appropriate for him, but not necessarily for you."

Bruce Lee

"The crowd mimics its heroes. This is a natural tendency, but there is no need for such mimicry. It is illogical for one who has not earned his master title to ape the complicated opening variations played by, say, a world champion."

Lajos Portisch (*How to Open a Chess Game*)

Players often think they cannot go far wrong by playing the variations used by a great player. Unfortunately they often do so and without the necessary research or understanding. The result is that what worked for Bobby Fischer or Garry Kasparov does not work for them. And they remain baffled as to the reason why.

It took me a while to learn to play 'my own game', but what exactly does that mean? It means that players should adopt lines which they have made their own by living with them over a period of time, analysing them either alone or with a partner and trying them in both practice games and competition. Little by little the contours of these lines are etched into the soul, weapons which function as an extension of the hand.

The following game was one of those which taught me this difficult lesson. Playing against a young American Grandmaster and specialist in the Benko Gambit, I aped a recent theoretical recommendation and was badly beaten.

Game 28
N.Davies-P.Wolff
Preston 1989
Benko Gambit

---

1 d4 ♘f6 2 c4 c5 3 d5 b5 4 cxb5 a6 5 e3 g6 6 ♘c3 ♗g7 7 a4 0-0 8 ♖a3 ♗b7 9 ♘h3

This move resulted from one of my attempts to get up to date with 'theory'; otherwise I would surely have put the knight on its natural f3-square. This variation was topical at the time of the game and 9 ♘h3 was touted as an improvement for White. But it becomes clear that Patrick Wolff had his own ideas on the matter.

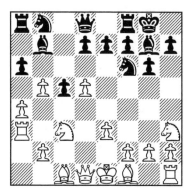

9...e6 10 ♘f4 e5!?

The temporary closing of the h8-a1 diagonal seems counter-intuitive but Black is using the knight's position to advance his e-pawn to e4.

The game that had 'inspired' me to play this line was B.Kouatly-J.Fedorowicz, Sesimbra 1987, which went 10...♗h6. Here I was ready to play Kouatly's suggested improvement of 11 e4! exd5 12 ♘fxd5 ♗xc1 13 ♘xf6+ ♕xf6 14 ♕xc1 ♖e8 15 ♗c4! ♗xe4 16 0-0, with a great game for White.

11 ♘h3

After 11 ♘d3 Black plays 11...♕e7! with the idea of meeting 12 e4 with 12...c4.

11...e4 12 ♘f4 d6 13 ♗e2 axb5 14 ♗xb5

In retrospect I should have played 14 axb5 ♘bd7 15 0-0, but the act of playing someone else's variation had disengaged my mind.

14...♘a6 15 0-0 ♘b4 16 ♗c4 ♕e7 17 ♕d2?!

After this artificial move Black ob-

tains a powerful attack. 17 ♗d2 would have been better, though Black is at least equal after 17...♕e5.

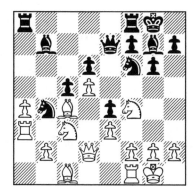

17...g5! 18 ♘fe2 ♘g4! 19 b3 ♕e5 20 g3 ♕f5

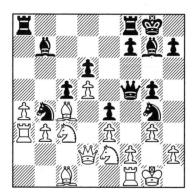

21 ♘xe4?!

Losing. 21 ♘b5 would have held on, but this is not a pleasant position for White.

21...♕xe4 22 f3 ♕xe3+ 23 ♕xe3 ♘xe3 24 ♗xe3 ♘c2 25 ♗c1 ♘xa3 26 ♗xa3 ♗a6 27 ♖c1 ♖fb8 0-1

Not one of my better days at the office.

23) Beware of lurking crocodiles

Crocodiles have survived for some 250 million years, making them one of the World's longest surviving species. As such their methods of survival are well worth studying. As far as hunting is concerned they are known to remain in or near water, just waiting for the return of suitable prey. This is evidently a very successful way to hunt that has stood the test of time.

This hunting method is also common on the chess board; players who are too predictable in their choice of watering hole are likely to find some crocs waiting there. For this reason a player needs to be careful about where they choose to drink, varying just enough to confuse waiting crocs.

Bobby Fischer learned this lesson during his 1972 match against Boris Spassky. For years he had played 1 e4 and used the Sozin Attack (6 ♗c4) against the Sicilian. But when he employed this line he found that crocodiles were lurking. It was only when he found new places to drink that he took charge of the match (see, for example, Game 22).

Game 29
R.Fischer-B.Spassky
World Championship
(4th game), Reykjavik 1972
Sicilian Defence

---

1 e4 c5 2 ♘f3 d6 3 d4 cxd4 4 ♘xd4 ♘f6 5 ♘c3 ♘c6 6 ♗c4 e6 7 ♗b3 ♗e7 8 ♗e3 0-0 9 0-0 a6 10 f4

(see following diagram)

10...♘xd4

This opening will have come as no surprise to Spassky as Fischer had reached the position after 10 f4 in several earlier games. We can therefore be quite confident that what follows is a

piece of Soviet preparation, crocodiles lurking by the watering hole.

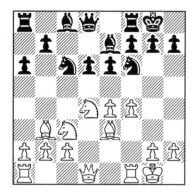

The alternatives had not produced satisfactory positions for Black. For example:

a) 10...♘a5 11 ♕f3 (11 g4 d5 12 e5 ♘d7 13 ♕f3 ♕c7 14 h4 ♘c4 was less convincing for White in R.Fischer-

L.Evans, New York 1958) 11...♕c7 (11...b5 12 e5 ♗b7 13 exf6 ♗xf3 14 fxe7 ♕xe7 15 ♖xf3 ♘c4 was the game R.Fischer-S.King, Westerly (simul) 1964, and here Fischer should have played a preliminary 16 ♗xc4 before playing 17 f5, as 16 f5 ♘xe3 was not good for him in the game) 12 g4 ♘xb3 13 axb3 ♖b8 14 g5 ♘d7 15 f5 ♘e5 16 ♕g3 and White had a strong initiative in R.Fischer-R.Cardoso, New York 1957.

b) 10...♗d7 11 ♕f3 ♖c8 12 f5 ♘xd4 13 ♗xd4 ♔h8 14 g4 ♘g8 15 ♖ad1 was good for White in R.Fischer-L.Limoh, Houston (simul) 1964.

11 ♗xd4 b5

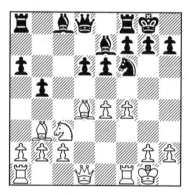

12 a3

After this passive move Black takes the initiative.

Later attempts to improve for White focussed on 12 e5, after which 12...dxe5 13 fxe5 ♘d7 14 ♘e4 ♗b7 15 ♘d6 ♗xd6 16 exd6 ♕g5 17 ♖f2! is far from clear: White has two bishops and a passed pawn on d6; Black has very active pieces and a firm blockade of that d6-pawn.

12...♗b7 13 ♕d3 a5!

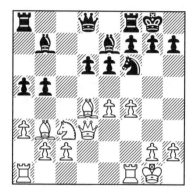

A strong move, with the threat of 14...b4. It works because 15 ♕xb5 can be met by 15...♗a6.

14 e5 dxe5 15 fxe5 ♘d7

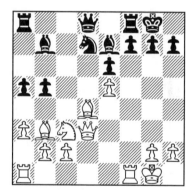

16 ♘xb5

White reasons that he might as well have a pawn for his troubles.

16 ♕xb5? would just lose the exchange after 16...♗a6, whilst 16 ♘e4 ♗xe4 17 ♕xe4 ♘c5 18 ♕e3 (18 ♗xc5 ♗xc5+ 19 ♔h1 ♕d4! is strong) 18...♘xb3 19 cxb3 ♖c8 gives Black the better game without any risk.

16...♘c5 17 ♗xc5

17 ♕e3 ♘xb3 18 ♕xb3 (and not 18

cxb3?? because of 18...♕d5 19 ♕e2 ♗c6 winning a piece) 18...a4 19 ♕d3 ♕d5 20 ♖f2 ♖fd8 gives Black more than enough for the pawn.

17...♗xc5+ 18 ♔h1 ♕g5

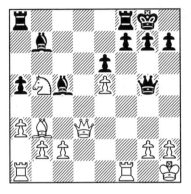

19 ♕e2?

White should probably have tried to bail out into an endgame with 19 ♕g3, after which 19...♕xg3 20 hxg3 ♗a6 (20...a4 21 ♗c4 ♖a5 22 ♘d6 is less good) 21 a4 ♗xb5 22 axb5 ♗d4 23 c3 ♗xe5 24 g4 ♖fd8 25 ♖fd1 ♗c7 is better for Black but probably drawn with best play.

19...♖ad8! 20 ♖ad1 ♖xd1 21 ♖xd1

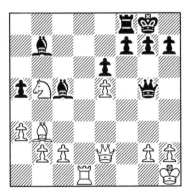

21...h5

Another interesting possibility was

21...♗e3!? intending 22...♗f4, although then White seems to hold with 22 ♘d6 ♗c6 23 ♘c4 ♗f4 24 ♔g1 ♕h4 25 h3 ♕g3 26 ♔f1 ♕h2 27 ♕f2 etc.

22 ♘d6 ♗a8 23 ♗c4 h4 24 h3

After 24 ♘e4 ♕xe5 25 ♘xc5 ♕xc5 26 h3 ♕f5!, Black would have a strong initiative.

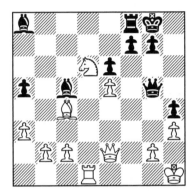

24...♗e3!

24...♕g3 25 ♘e4 ♕xe5 26 ♘xc5 ♕xc5 gives White an extra tempo when compared with the previous note.

25 ♕g4 ♕xe5

With White's king in danger it makes sense to keep the queens on.

26 ♕xh4 g5!

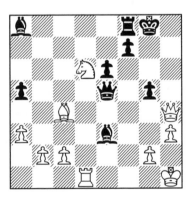

27 ♕g4 ♗c5

After 27...♖d8 White can play 28 ♘xf7! when 28...♖xd1+ 29 ♕xd1 ♕e4 (29...♔xf7 30 ♕d7+ draws) 30 ♗f1 (30 ♕f1 ♕xg2+ 31 ♕xg2 ♗xg2+ 32 ♔xg2 ♔xf7 is also drawn) 30...♔xf7 31 ♕d7+ ♔f6 32 ♕d8+ ♔e5 33 ♕c7+! leads to a draw by perpetual check.

28 ♘b5 ♔g7 29 ♘d4

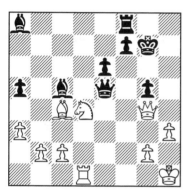

29...♖h8

29...♗d6 is met by 30 ♘f5+!, as pointed out by Purdy.

Several commentators suggested that Black should play 29...♖d8!? in order to force 30 c3 (not 30 ♘f5+? because of 30...♔f6!!) and only then play 30...♖h8. The idea of course is to cut out White's defensive resource based on 32 ♕c3, but White has another defensive resource: 31 ♗xe6! ♗xd4 (31...fxe6 32 ♘xe6+ ♔f6 33 ♘xc5 ♕xc5

34 ♕d7! even wins for White) 32 cxd4! ♕xe6 33 ♕xg5+ ♕g6 34 ♕e5+ ♔h7 35 d5 shuts the bishop on a8 out of the game, with reasonable prospects for White.

30 ♘f3 ♗xf3 31 ♕xf3

31...♗d6?

Allowing White to escape. Timman found a better line for Black here in 31...♖h4!, after which 32 ♖f1 ♖f4 33 ♕e2 ♖xf1+ 34 ♕xf1 ♗d6 35 ♔g1?! (35 ♕g1 would hang on but it's very unpleasant for White after 35...♕xb2) 35...♕h2+ 36 ♔f2 ♕f4+ 37 ♔g1 ♕d4+ 38 ♔h1 ♕xb2 would leave White in desperate trouble.

32 ♕c3! ♕xc3 33 bxc3 ♗e5 34 ♖d7 ♔f6 35 ♔g1 ♗xc3 36 ♗e2 ♗e5 37 ♔f1 ♖c8 38 ♗h5 ♖c7 39 ♖xc7 ♗xc7 40 a4 ♔e7 41 ♔e2 f5 42 ♔d3 ♗e5 43 c4 ♔d6 44 ♗f7 ♗g3 45 c5+ 1-0

24) Try to meet threats with developing moves

"This reminds me of a rule I know very well because I made it up: When you are caught in an opening you don't know, play healthy developing moves!"

Bent Larsen (*How to Open a Chess Game*)

"For the practical needs of chess the concept 'compensation' suffices. If the advantages held by my opponent are compensated for by my advantages, the position is balanced. Then no attack, the intent of which is to win – so argues Steinitz – must be undertaken. The idea of balance is enough to convince us that balanced positions with best play on either side must lead again and again to balanced positions."

Emanuel Lasker (*Lasker's Manual of Chess*)

Over the years I've found these two concepts to be of immense value; if someone does not make any particularly bad moves they should not get into trouble, and this in turn can give them faith in their position even when their opponent is creating threats or comes up with a surprise. This faith in the justice of the chess board leads the search for crisp, sensible replies in often trying circumstances.

The following game was one of the best from my teenage years, a sharply conducted attack against my opponent's king. But with more faith in his earlier moves, my opponent might well have investigated 10...♗e7 more deeply and seen the route to salvation. It does not make sense that Black should be lost and the justice of the chess board would have come shining through.

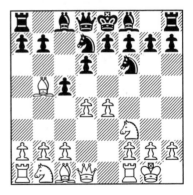

Game 30
N.Davies-C.Baljon
Lloyds Bank Masters,
London 1980
Sicilian Defence

---

1 e4 c5 2 ♘f3 d6 3 ♗b5+ ♘d7 4 d4 ♘gf6 5 0-0!?

(see following diagram)

This interesting gambit started to

appear when they found that 5 ♘c3 cxd4 6 ♕xd4 e5 7 ♕d3 h6 (preventing 8 ♗g5) was very reasonable for Black. Now White can meet 5...cxd4 6 ♕xd4 e5 7 ♕d3 h6 with 8 c4!.

5...♘xe4

Taking the pawn looks critical. After all, it is an important centre pawn.

6 ♕e2 ♘ef6 7 dxc5 dxc5 8 ♖d1

Setting up a pin along the d-file. This position is evidently very dangerous for Black, but what has he done that's so very wrong?

8...e6 9 ♗g5 h6 10 ♗h4

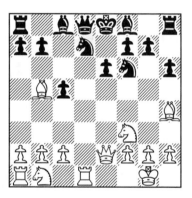

10...♕b6?

Whereas taking a centre pawn logically justifies using some time, developing the queen like this does not. Black was evidently worried about the pin along the d-file but this steps out of the frying pan directly into the fire.

It turns out that natural development was the way for Black to go, and here he could play the cold-blooded 10...♗e7! after which 11 ♘e5 0-0 12 ♗xf6 ♗xf6 13 ♘xd7 (13 ♗xd7 ♗xe5 14 ♕xe5 ♗xd7 15 ♕xc5 b6 16 ♕e5 f6 17 ♕e4 ♕c7 is just fine for Black)

13...♗xd7 14 ♖xd7 ♕c8 leaves White facing the dual threats of 15...♗xb2 and 15...a6. A possible sequel is 15 ♖d1 ♗xb2 16 ♘d2 ♗xa1 17 ♖xa1 ♖d8, and with a rook and two pawns for two minor pieces Black is certainly no worse.

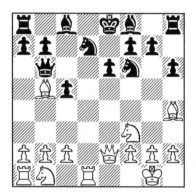

11 ♘a3

Threatening to gain further time on Black's queen with 12 ♘c4, the point being that 12...♕xb5 would lose the queen to 13 ♘d6+.

11...a6 12 ♗xd7+ ♗xd7 13 ♘c4 ♕a7

After 13...♕c7 White plays 14 ♗g3, which is very unpleasant.

14 ♘ce5

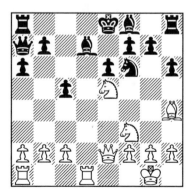

14...♗c8

Black undevelops one of the few pieces that he has developed, but in this position there's a distinct lack of good moves. The alternatives are refuted as follows:

a) 14...♗c6 15 ♘xf7 ♔xf7 (15...♗xf3 is answered by 16 ♕xe6+) 16 ♘e5+ ♔g8 (if 16...♔e7 then 17 ♘g6+; or 16...♔e8 17 ♗xf6 gxf6 18 ♕h5+ ♔e7 19 ♕f7 mate) 17 ♗xf6 gxf6 18 ♕g4+ ♗g7 19 ♕xe6+ ♔h7 20 ♘xc6 bxc6 21 ♖d7 ♕b8 (21...♕b6 22 ♕f5+ ♔g8 23 ♕g6 ♖h7 24 ♖e1 wins) 22 ♕f5+ ♔g8 23 ♖ad1 ♕f8 (on 23...♕e8 there follows 24 ♖xg7+ ♔xg7 25 ♖d7+ ♕xd7 26 ♕xd7+ and Black's pawn weaknesses spell doom; and if 23...♕e5 White wins with 24 ♕g6 ♖h7 25 ♖d8+ followed by mate) 24 ♕e6+ ♔h7 25 ♖f7 ♕e8 26 ♖dd7 ♖g8 27 ♕f5+ ♔h8 28 ♖fe7 ♕f8 29 ♕g6 and the threat of 30 ♕xh6+ ♗xh6 31 ♖h7 mate is decisive.

b) 14...♖d8 15 ♘xf7 ♔xf7 16 ♘e5+ ♔g8 (16...♔e7 is answered by 17 ♘g6+ followed by taking the rook on h8, and 16...♔e8 by 17 ♗xf6 gxf6 18 ♕h5+ followed by mate on f7) 17 ♗xf6 gxf6 18 ♘xd7 ♔f7 19 ♘e5+ and White wins.

15 ♘xf7! ♔xf7 16 ♘e5+

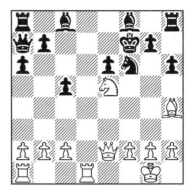

16...♔g8

On 16...♔e8 White can force mate with 17 ♕h5+ ♘xh5 18 ♖d8, while 16...♔e7 is met by 17 ♕h5 threatening mate on f7.

17 ♗xf6 b5

Or 17...gxf6 18 ♕g4+ ♗g7 19 ♖d8+ ♔h7 20 ♕g6 mate.

18 ♕g4 ♕c7 19 ♖d8 h5 20 ♕g5 ♖h6 21 ♖xf8+ ♔xf8 22 ♗xg7+ ♕xg7 23 ♕d8 mate (1-0)

25) Engage the mind

"The Hacker has a different attitude. After sort of getting the hang of a thing, he or she is willing to stay on the plateau indefinitely. He doesn't mind skipping stages essential to the development of mastery if he can just go out and hack around with fellow hackers. He's the physician or teacher who doesn't bother going to professional meetings, the tennis player who develops a solid forehand and figures he can make do with a ragged backhand. At work, he does only enough to get by, leaves on time or early, takes every break, talks instead of doing his job, and wonders why he doesn't get promoted."

George Leonard (*Mastery*)

Bronstein remarked about a certain Soviet champion that he played the opening as if he was 'dealing the cards'. Even at such a high level this represents the attitude of a hacker, someone who has found something that more or less works and repeats it like an automaton. And as Bronstein pointed out, it is a weakness.

Fischer often played the opening quite thoughtfully in spite of his extensive knowledge of the openings he played. Despite this he was a very quick player overall because of his acceleration in the early middlegame. This use of time can be quite natural if players use the opening to engage their minds. Indeed the king of time-trouble, Samuel Reshevsky, stated that the time he used in the opening and early middlegame brought him in tune with the position so that he could play quickly later on. Whilst I am not recommending that players go as far as Reshevsky in this matter, his point of view is worth noting. The mind should be engaged.

The following game should serve as a warning to those who play the opening automatically. My opponent was playing his moves rather nonchalantly so I figured a little trap was in order:

Game 31
N.Davies-D.Knox
Bolton (rapidplay) 2003
Irregular Defence

---

1 ♘f3 h6 2 e4 a6

Had I lost this game I would have been shamed for all eternity. Black is using the same 'strategy' that Tony Miles adopted in his win over Karpov with 1 e4 a6. But since that no longer insults people so much, both rook's pawns need to be pushed to create the same effect. Facing this, I resolved to keep calm and try to develop my pieces sensibly.

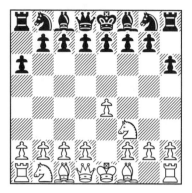

3 d4 c6 4 ♗d3 d5

In a Caro-Kann type set-up the lost tempi are not as critical as in open games. But obviously White is going to be better here if he keeps his head.

5 ♘bd2 dxe4 6 ♘xe4 ♗g4 7 0-0 ♘d7

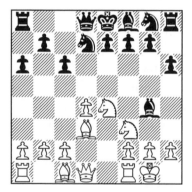

8 ♖e1

A really sly move which is thinly veiled by sensibly occupying the half-open e-file. From an objective point of view there might have been better moves but I was curious to see if Black would continue moving quickly.

8...♘gf6??

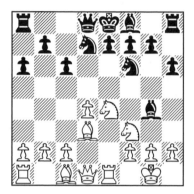

After picking up the knight he suddenly saw my threat, but it was too late. Sportingly my opponent allowed me to deliver mate, which does not happen too often these days.

9 ♘d6 mate (1-0)

26) In open positions develop quickly

"Let us examine the open game more closely from the point of view of general characteristics. Black proclaims by his symmetrical reply 1...e5; his firm decision to cross swords as quickly as possible with his adversary and (in spite of 'the move') to meet him on an equal footing in the centre of the board, whereas a passive reply such as a King's or Queen's Fianchetto (1...g6 or 1...b6) would allow White to occupy the centre immediately and for good by 2 d4.

"After the typical moves 1 e4 e5; we frequently see a lively struggle, seeking in particular to gain the mastery of the centre. Each move in the initial stage must be telling, in other words, it must contain some threat of an immediate nature (attack on a pawn, an effective pin of a piece, unpinning, counter-attack, etc.), and a game of chess of this type resembles an encounter between two fencers where thrust and parry follow and offset each other."

Savielly Tartakower (*A Breviary of Chess*)

Here's a classic example which illustrates the danger of falling behind in development. Black loses time in the opening and is drastically punished.

> *Game 32*
> **De Legall-Saint Brie**
> Paris 1750
> *Philidor Defence*

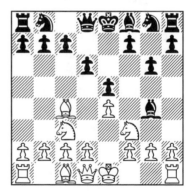

1 e4 e5 2 ♘f3 d6 3 ♗c4 ♗g4

It's better to delay the development of this bishop, though taken on its own this would be a playable move for Black.

4 ♘c3 g6??

In closed, blocked positions it's a lot easier to get away with such moves. Here, with the c4-bishop pointing directly at f7, it represents a fatal loss of time.

5 ♘xe5! ♗xd1??

Losing immediately. Black had to try 5...dxe5 when after 6 ♕xg4 he's a pawn down but could at least continue the game.

6 ♗xf7+ ♔e7 7 ♘d5 mate (1-0)

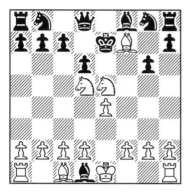

Open positions don't just arise after the moves 1 e4 e5, and sometimes these two moves lead to closed games in the case, for example, of the Closed Variation of the Ruy Lopez (1 e4 e5 2 ♘f3 ♘c6 3 ♗b5 a6 4 ♗a4 ♘f6 5 0-0 ♗e7 6 ♖e1 b5 7 ♗b3 d6 8 c3 0-0 9 h3 and now 9...♘a5 10 ♗c2 c5 11 d4 ♕c7 12 ♘bd2 ♘c6 13 d5 brings about a closed centre). Yet these two moves have most commonly been associated with sharp, open play in which speedy development needs to be emphasized.

If a player has a lead in development in a closed position, he should consider means of opening things up. The following game, taken from the second Fischer-Spassky match, is a classic example of this strategy:

> ### Game 33
> **R.Fischer-B.Spassky**
> Sveti Stefan/Belgrade
> (11th matchgame) 1992
> *Sicilian Defence*

1 e4 c5 2 ♘f3 ♘c6 3 ♗b5

Earlier in his career Fischer almost always played 3 d4 and was known for his deep theoretical knowledge in the lines that he played. Of course that was back in the 1960s and early 1970s, before the advent of computers.

3...g6 4 ♗xc6 bxc6

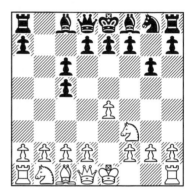

4...dxc6 is seen more often but capturing towards the centre will obviously be of interest.

5 0-0 ♗g7 6 ♖e1

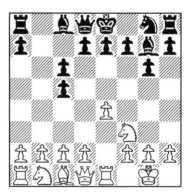

6...e5

Black has tried a few other moves here, delaying occupation of the centre whilst trying to catch up in development. Here are some recent examples:

a) 6...♘h6 7 c3 0-0 8 d4 ♕b6 9 h3 f6 10 b3 cxd4 11 cxd4 ♘f7 12 ♘bd2 d6 13 ♗b2 ♗d7 gave Black a solid game in V.Baklan-S.Maze, Reykjavik 2008.

b) 6...f6 7 c3 ♘h6 8 d4 cxd4 9 cxd4 ♘f7 10 b3 0-0 11 ♘bd2 was the game E.Van den Doel-J.Van der Wiel, Leiden 2008, and now 11...d6 (rather than the game's 11...a5) 12 ♗b2 ♗d7 would have been similar to Baklan-Maze, above.

c) 6...♘f6 7 e5 ♘d5 8 c4 ♘c7 9 d4 cxd4 10 ♕xd4 0-0 11 ♕h4 f6 12 exf6 exf6 13 b3 ♘e6 14 ♗b2 g5 15 ♕e4 d5 16 ♕c2 d4 17 ♕e4 ♖b8 was agreed drawn in this interesting position in S.Rublevsky-E.Sutovsky, Poikovsky 2008.

7 b4!?

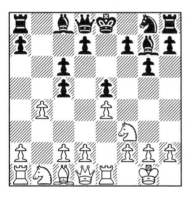

A new move by Fischer, and a very interesting one. With Black being behind in development, White adopts the old fashioned strategy of opening lines up for his pieces.

7...cxb4 8 a3 c5

If Black accepts the pawn with 8...bxa3 White should probably recapture with the knight so as to play ♘a3-

c4 and ♗c1-a3 or ♗c1-f4. For example, 9 ♘xa3 d6 10 d4 exd4 11 ♗f4 ♘e7 12 ♘c4 0-0 13 ♘xd6 recovers one of the pawns and gets excellent compensation for the other.

Black could try and play it safe with 8...b3 but White seems to be better after 9 cxb3 ♘e7 10 ♗b2 d6 11 d4.

9 axb4 cxb4 10 d4 exd4 11 ♗b2 d6

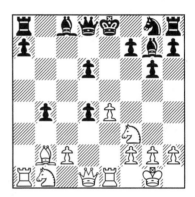

12 ♘xd4

Another possibility was 12 ♗xd4 when 12...♘f6 13 c3! (13 e5 dxe5 14 ♖xe5+ ♗e6 would be good for Black) 13...0-0 (13...bxc3 14 e5 dxe5 15 ♕a4+ ♗d7 16 ♖xe5+ would prevent Black from castling) 14 cxb4 would be slightly better for White.

12...♕d7

After the game Spassky preferred 12...♕b6 but then 13 ♘d2! ♗xd4 14 ♘c4 ♗xf2+ 15 ♔h1 ♕c5 16 ♘xd6+ ♔e7 17 ♖f1 ♕xd6 18 ♕f3! would give White a vitriolic attack for the sacrificed material.

13 ♘d2 ♗b7

13...♘e7 14 ♘c4 0-0 15 ♘b6 would win the exchange.

14 ♘c4

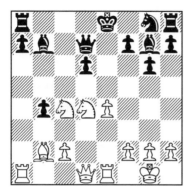

14...♘h6

White can also play 15 ♘f5! after 14...♘e7. For example, 15...♗xb2 16 ♘fxd6+ ♚f8 17 ♘xb2 ♚g8 18 ♘bc4 gives White a tremendous initiative for the pawn deficit, as Black is still playing without his king's rook.

15 ♘f5! ♗xb2 16 ♘cxd6+ ♚f8 17 ♘xh6 f6?

Missing Fischer's 21st move.

Black should have tried 17...♗xa1 18 ♕xa1 ♕xd6 19 ♕xh8+ ♚e7 20 ♕xh7 ♖f8 when he at least has a strong bishop and passed a-pawn to compensate him for his king's position.

18 ♘df7! ♕xd1 19 ♖axd1 ♚e7 20 ♘xh8 ♖xh8 21 ♘f5+!

This thunderbolt decides the game in White's favour, as he forces off one of Black's bishops. Without this possibility the position would have offered Black very reasonable prospects.

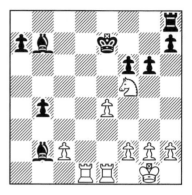

21...gxf5

After 21...♚e6, 22 ♖d6+ ♚e5 (22...♚f7 23 ♖d7+ wins the bishop on b7) 23 ♖d7 ♗c6 24 ♖e7+ ♚f4 25 g3+ ♚g4 26 ♘e3+ would win Black's a7-pawn and leave his king in peril.

22 exf5+ ♗e5 23 f4 ♖c8 24 fxe5 ♖xc2 25 e6 ♗c6

25...♖xg2+ is nothing for Black after 26 ♚f1.

26 ♖c1 ♖xc1 27 ♖xc1 ♚d6 28 ♖d1+ ♚e5 29 e7 a5 30 ♖c1! ♗d7 31 ♖c5+ ♚d4 32 ♖xa5 b3 33 ♖a7 ♗e8 34 ♖b7 ♚c3 35 ♚f2 b2 36 ♚e3 ♗f7 37 g4 ♚c2 38 ♚d4 b1♕ 39 ♖xb1 ♚xb1 40 ♚c5 ♚c2 41 ♚d6 1-0

27) In closed positions develop well

Closed positions do not require the same speedy development as open ones. Certainly it can be dangerous to develop in too tardy a fashion in case the position suddenly gets opened up. But generally speaking it is better to emphasize pawn structure and *quality* rather than *quantity* of development. The aim should be to place the pieces in such a way that they will be effective in the coming middlegame.

This means that the study of complete games is far more important in closed openings; to know where the pieces belong it's important to see lots of middlegame action. And a good way to do this is to search a computer database for strong players playing the position you want to understand better, print the games out and then go through them with a real board and pieces. The experience of moving pieces around a board makes chess material far more memorable than using a computer screen.

How many games should one go through in this manner? Well Victor Korchnoi played through some 10,000 games opening with 1 d4 before switching to this opening move from 1 e4, but this huge number may be difficult for most people to find time for. I would suggest starting out by going through 10 games for each new opening and then gradually building on that. After a few years of study and practice a player will normally have a decent grasp of an opening.

The following game shows the value of pawn structure and quality of development in a closed opening. Black developed his pieces on squares that would have been highly effective in an open game. But here the flexibility of White's pawn structure plus the latent power of his pieces was far more important.

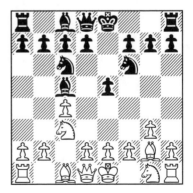

> *Game 34*
> **M.Taimanov-V.Hort**
> Tallinn 1975
> *English Opening*

1 c4 e5 2 ♘c3 ♘c6 3 g3 ♘f6 4 ♗g2 ♗c5

A 'sensible' looking developing move of the type that is often recommended in beginners' books.

Yet here it is of questionable value because the position is closed and it is not clear that the bishop will have such great prospects on this square.

5 e3 d6

Black can try to shake off the coming grip with 5...d5!?, though if White keeps a cool head it does not solve Black's opening problems. Vlad Tomescu played this way against me at Saint Vincent in 1999, but after 6 cxd5 ♘b4 7 d3 ♘bxd5 8 ♘xd5 ♘xd5 9 ♘f3 ♗b4+ 10 ♗d2 ♗xd2+ 11 ♕xd2 ♕e7 12 0-0 c6 13 e4 ♘b6 14 ♕c3 f6 15 d4 exd4 16 ♘xd4 I stood better and went on to win.

6 a3 ♗e6?!

There's a case for stopping White's queenside expansion with 6...a5.

7 b4 ♗b6 8 d3 ♕d7 9 h3

The immediate 9 ♘ge2?! is answered by 9...♗h3.

9...0-0 10 ♘ge2

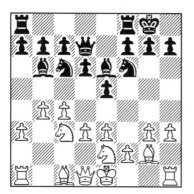

10...♘d8

Rightly playing to get more of a grip on the centre with pawns – Black wants to play ...c7-c6 followed by ...♗b6-c7. The problem Black has here

is that his dark-squared bishop gets exchanged before it can tuck into the c7-square.

11 ♘a4! c6 12 ♘xb6 axb6 13 ♗b2 ♘e8

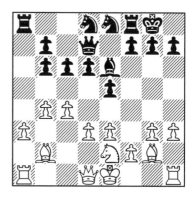

14 f4

Grabbing more space, this time on the kingside.

14...f6 15 g4 ♔h8?

Black makes room for his bishop to drop back to g8, but after White's simple reply he can't carry out this plan. Accordingly it would have been better to play 15...♘c7.

16 0-0 ♕e7

16...♗g8? loses a pawn to 17 fxe5 dxe5 18 ♗xe5 because the f6-pawn is pinned against Black's rook on f8.

17 ♕e1

The queen heads for the kingside in order to menace Black's king.

17...♗f7 18 ♘g3 ♗g6 19 ♖d1 ♘c7

Black could exchange queens here with 19...exf4 20 exf4 ♕xe1 but after 21 ♖fxe1 he would have to endure a horrific endgame with White being ready to bring a rook to e7.

20 ♕f2 b5 21 c5!

Setting fire to the supports of the

e5-pawn, which in turn is Black's means of keeping the a1-h8 diagonal closed.

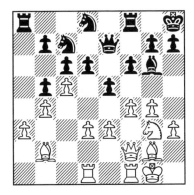

21...exf4

After 21...d5 22 fxe5 Black cannot recapture.

22 exf4 h6

Or if 22...dxc5 there follows 23 ♖fe1 ♕d7 24 f5 ♗f7 25 g5! with a powerful attack.

23 ♗e4! ♗xe4 24 cxd6 ♕xd6 25 dxe4 ♕e6 26 e5! fxe5 27 ♗xe5 ♘d5 28 ♕b2 ♕f7 29 ♘h5!

The right way to gang up on the g7-

pawn. 29 ♘f5?! ♘e6 30 ♘xh6 ♕g6 is less clear.

29...♖g8 30 f5

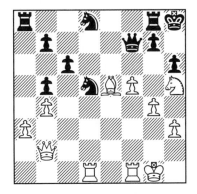

30...b6

30...♘e3 is answered by 31 ♕c1! ♘xd1 32 ♕xh6 mate.

31 ♖fe1 ♘b7

31...♔h7 is no better because of 32 ♗xg7! ♖xg7 33 ♖xd5! cxd5 34 ♘f6+ ♔h8 35 ♖e8+ etc, while 31...♖a7 is demolished by the line 32 ♗xg7+ ♖xg7 33 ♖xd5 cxd5 34 ♘xg7 ♕xg7 35 ♖e8+ ♔h7 36 f6.

32 ♕c1! ♔h7 33 ♕xc6 1-0

28) Centralize

The simplest way to understand the importance of the centre is to compare the powers of the pieces on various different squares. A knight in the centre can move to as many as eight squares; in the corner just two. A centralized bishop can sometimes move to thirteen; in a corner just seven. A centralized queen can cover 27; in the corner a maximum of 21. This makes the centre the high ground of the chess board and the most valuable piece of terrain to occupy.

Because of the greater effect of centralized pieces, it was originally thought that a player should go all out to occupy the centre directly, with pawns and then pieces. There are, however, a number of caveats to this idea. For example, the occupation of the centre could be temporary if the occupying forces can be undermined or driven back, or if occupation with pawns does not lend itself to the support of an army's pieces. This lends great complexity to the issue, which these days tends to be considered on a case-by-case basis.

The following two games are won by centralization but feature quite different angles on this theme. In the first the great Bent Larsen artfully uses a central pawn preponderance gained early on to squeeze his opponent to death. The second is one of my own in which I use the hypermodern strategy of whittling away White's central pawns from the side and then finally occupying the centre myself.

Game 35
B.Larsen-L.Lengyel
Amsterdam Interzonal 1964
Vienna Game

---

1 e4 e5 2 ♗c4 ♘f6 3 ♘c3 ♘c6 4 d3 ♗b4 5 ♘f3 d6 6 0-0 ♗xc3 7 bxc3 ♘a5

I learned the lesson of this game rather better when I chose to play this position with Black against Larsen in London, 1989. After 7...♗g4 8 h3 ♗h5 9 ♗b3 ♘d7 10 ♗e3 ♕e7 11 ♖b1 ♘d8 12 ♔h2 f6 13 ♕d2 ♗f7 14 ♘h4 g6 15 f4 ♗xb3 16 axb3 White was clearly better.

8 ♗b3 ♘xb3 9 axb3

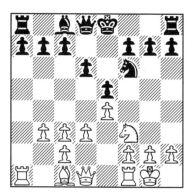

White has contracted a set of doubled pawns on the c-file but in no way are they weak. In fact White's pawns

---

form a single island from b3 to h2 which helps to control the centre. As the game develops we see Larsen nurture and increase this central control until the island produces a passed pawn.

9...0-0 10 c4 ♕e7 11 ♘d2 ♘d7 12 ♕h5 ♘c5 13 f4

Commencing the process of whittling away Black central pawns. Black now gets to exchange queens but this doesn't change the basic structure.

13...exf4 14 ♖xf4 ♕e5 15 ♕xe5 dxe5 16 ♖f2 ♘e6 17 ♘f3 f6 18 ♗e3 a6 19 ♘h4 ♗d7 20 ♘f5 ♖ae8 21 h3 ♖f7 22 ♔h2 ♘f8 23 g4 ♘g6 24 ♘g3 ♘e7 25 ♖af1 ♗e6 26 ♘e2

It looks as if White has been building up for 26 g5 but this would have achieved very little apart from letting Black exchange a pair of rooks. His real goal has been to stop Black freeing himself with ...f7-f5.

26...♘c6 27 ♔g3 ♘b8 28 ♘c3 c6

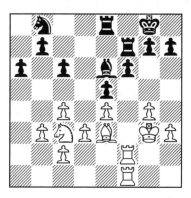

Preventing White's knight from landing on d5 but creating weaknesses on the dark squares.

29 c5! ♘d7 30 ♘a4 ♖d8 31 h4 ♖df8 32

♘b2 ♖c8 33 ♖a1

Commencing an odd-looking but very effective manoeuvre. White's rook is headed for b4 from where it will attack Black's b7-pawn whilst defending b3. The latter is important because White ultimately wants to play c2-c3 and d3-d4.

33...♔f8 34 ♖a4 ♔e8 35 ♖b4 ♖c7 36 c3

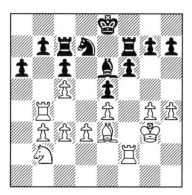

White finally gets ready for the advance of the centre pawns. This prompts Black to look for counterplay, but in doing so he further weakens his position.

36...g6?

It's not clear how White would have proceeded after 36...♔d8 because 37 d4 ♖e7 puts some latent pressure against e4. In his notes to the game Larsen wrote that he would probably have played some quiet moves rather than undertake immediate action.

37 d4 h5?

Making matters worse, but after his last move Black can no longer sit still.

After 37...f5 there would have followed 38 gxf5 gxf5 39 exf5 ♗xf5 40 ♘c4! intending to jump into d6.

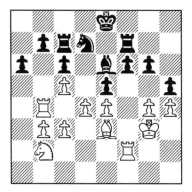

38 g5 fxg5

After 38...f5 39 exf5 ♖xf5 40 ♖xf5 gxf5 (or 40...♗xf5 41 ♘c4) 41 dxe5 the position is highly unpleasant for Black.

39 ♗xg5 exd4 40 ♖xf7 ♔xf7 41 cxd4

The game was adjourned at this point with White holding a huge advantage.

41...♘f6 42 ♔f4 a5 43 ♖a4 ♗xb3 44 ♖xa5 ♘g4 45 ♖a3 ♗e6 46 ♘d3 ♔g7 47 ♘e5!

Exchanging off Black's main protector of the dark squares. And note that opposite-coloured bishops are far from drawish when there are still rooks on the board.

47...♖c8 48 ♗e7 ♖e8 49 ♗d6 ♘xe5 50 ♗xe5+ ♔f7 51 ♔g5 ♗g4 52 ♖a1 ♖e6 53 ♖b1 ♖e7 54 ♖f1+ ♔e8 55 ♔xg6

Finally a gain of material, and in turn Black's h-pawn now becomes vulnerable.

55...♔d7 56 ♖f4 ♗e2 57 ♗d6 ♖e6+ 58 ♔g5 ♗d3 59 ♗e5 ♗e2 60 ♖f2 ♗d3 61 ♔f4 ♖g6 62 ♔e3 ♗c4 63 ♖f5 ♖g1 64 ♖xh5 ♖e1+ 65 ♔f4 ♗d3 66 ♖h7+ ♔e6

Allowing a decisive tactical finesse. 66...♔e8 67 ♖xb7 would also be an easy win for White.

67 d5+ cxd5 68 exd5+ ♔xd5 69 ♖d7+ 1-0

Black resigned because of 69...♔c4 70 ♖d4+ ♔c3 71 ♖e4+ ♔d2 72 ♗c3+ etc.

Game 36
J.Jackova-N.Davies
British League 2005
Modern Defence

---

1 e4 g6 2 d4 d6 3 ♘f3 ♗g7 4 ♗c4 ♘f6 5 ♕e2 0-0 6 e5 ♘e8 7 h3

This prevents ...♗c8-g4 but feels a bit slow. The following year my opponent improved on her play with 7 0-0, the game J.Jackova-V.Hort, Prague 2006, continuing 7...♘c6 (7...♗g4 8 ♖d1 would keep things under control) 8 h3 d5 9 ♗b5 ♗d7 10 c3 a6 11 ♗d3 ♕c8 12 ♖e1 ♗f5 13 ♗xf5 ♕xf5 14 ♘bd2 with White for choice because of her space advantage.

7...c5! 8 dxc5

White should probably just protect the d4-pawn with 8 c3. For example, 8...♘c7 9 dxc5 (only now) 9...d5 10 ♗d3

♘e6 11 ♗e3 ♘d7 12 0-0 ♕c7 13 c4 dxc4 14 ♗xc4 ♘xe5 was about equal in P.Negi-T.Hillarp Persson, Malmo 2007.

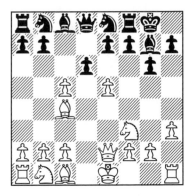

8...dxe5 9 0-0 ♘c6 10 c3 ♗f5

Despite the fact that Black did not initially occupy the centre, he now has a controlling interest by virtue of his two e-pawns.

11 ♘a3 ♘c7 12 ♖d1 ♕c8 13 ♗g5 ♗e6

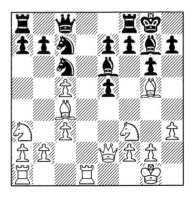

14 ♕e3?!

I think that my opponent mis-assessed the position around this point, believing she held the advantage when in fact the position is very dangerous for White. Putting the queen on e3 evidently envisages conjuring up some

play on the kingside, but it is Black's mass of kingside pawns that is the more important factor there.

14...f5! 15 b4 ♗xc4 16 ♘xc4 ♕e6

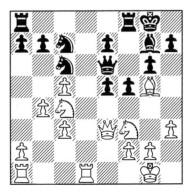

Centralizing the queen.

17 ♘a3 a6 18 ♕e2 e4 19 ♘d4 ♘xd4 20 cxd4 ♘d5

And now the knight comes to a powerful central outpost. Note that such possibilities are linked to the undermining of White's central pawns with 7...c5!.

21 ♕c4 ♖ad8

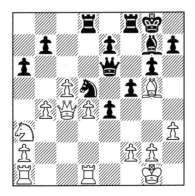

Continuing the centralization policy; now it's the rook.

22 b5

22 ♗c1 was better, stopping the bishop being trapped with 22...f4. Of course such moves are difficult to play, especially if the player concerned recently felt she stood better.

22...f4 23 bxa6 bxa6 24 c6 ♖f5

There's nowhere for the g5-bishop to go, but White had hoped for some tactical possibilities based on the passed c-pawn.

25 ♖ab1

After 25 ♗h4 ♖h5 26 g3, one good way to play it would be 26...♕xh3.

25...♖xg5 26 c7 ♖c8 27 ♖b8 ♗f8

The simple end to White's counterplay, though there is one more trick left in the game.

28 ♕b3 ♖xc7 29 ♘c4

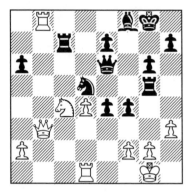

29...♖xc4! 30 ♕xc4 ♖xg2+ 0-1

White is losing her queen after the simple combination 30...♖xg2+ 31 ♔xg2 ♘e3+ etc.

29) Develop knights and the king's bishop early

"Contrary to the opinion which prevailed in ancient times, (an opinion supported also by Philidor), we prefer, today, to bring out the King's Knight before the corresponding Bishop, the reason being that the Knight will seldom be content with a permanent post, but will soon undertake bold and fresh manoeuvres, whereas the Bishop is likely to rest satisfied with the diagonal selected and can then remain on his post for a fairly long space of time.

"It is better therefore to leave until a little later the important choice of a field of action for the Bishops, and let it be then the more efficacious and definitive. The principle of delaying – be it even for only one move – our choice, will add to the elasticity of our fighting forces and this applies equally to castling."

Savielly Tartakower (*A Breviary of Chess*)

Many beginners' books tout the development of knights before bishops with the development of the rooks and queen following on afterwards. Whilst most players are aware that this is an oversimplification there is often a residual habit to develop the pieces rather mechanically. On occasion I've even caught myself thinking this way.

After watching my play in the following game, David Bronstein drew my attention to the fact that the queen's bishop is often developed quite late in the game. He did not particularly like my 15...♗f5, sensing that it was a somewhat hackneyed approach that was rooted in the old rules. In retrospect I agree, and I've been on the lookout for this kind of error in the games of other players.

Game 37
A.Neffe-N.Davies
Wrexham 1995
King's Indian Defence

---

1 e4 g6 2 d4 ♗g7 3 c4 d6 4 ♘c3 a6 5 h3 ♘f6

I would now prefer 5...c6 in this position; for example, 6 ♘f3 b5 7 a3 ♘d7 8 ♗e3 ♖b8 9 c5 dxc5 10 dxc5 ♕c7 11 ♕d2

♘gf6 was okay for Black in R.Vera-A.Zlochevskij, Porto San Giorgio 1998.

6 ♗g5

I've also had 6 ♘f3 played against me in a couple of games. Black has some problems there which stem from the danger of White playing e4-e5. This is why I believe it's better to delay ...♘g8-f6.

6...0-0 7 a4?!

A gratuitous weakening of White's queenside, especially given that Black was not even 'threatening' ...b7-b5. Black's reply is rather standard, simply taking the b4-square for later occupation by a knight.

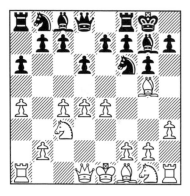

7...a5 8 f4

The kind of move that I'm always happy to see. Pawns do not move backwards, so multiple pawn advances can create serious long-term weaknesses.

8...c6 9 ♘f3 ♘h5!

Threatening both the f4-pawn (with 10...f6) and preparing to hop into the hole on g3. White's position is already looking very exposed.

10 ♕d2 d5!?

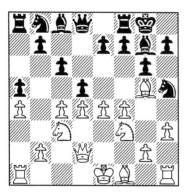

I decided to try and open it up, and didn't mind sacrificing a pawn to do it.

11 ♗d3

On 11 exd5 there are several attractive possibilities: for example, 11...♘g3 12 ♖g1 cxd5 13 ♘xd5 ♘c6 14 ♗d3 ♘f5 15 ♗xf5 ♗xf5 intending 16...♗e6 or 16...♗e4, which will recover the pawn with the better game.

11...♘g3 12 ♖g1 dxe4 13 ♗xe4

13 ♘xe4 ♘f5 puts White's d4-pawn in trouble.

13...♘a6 14 ♗h4 ♘xe4 15 ♘xe4

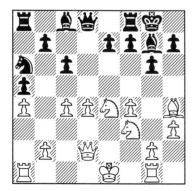

15...♗f5?!

Here's the move that Bronstein drew my attention to; he felt it was development for the sake of it. 15...♘b4 is probably a better choice, leaving the queen's bishop at home for yet another move.

16 ♘g3 ♗e6 17 ♖c1 ♕b6 18 f5!?

White gives up a pawn to try and get some counterplay. In the event the pawn is more valuable than the play White generates, but this is the kind of argument that validates Bronstein's view about 15...♗f5 being less than optimal.

18...♗xf5 19 ♘xf5 gxf5 20 g4 f4

This move manages to keep the g-file closed.

21 ♕xf4 ♕xb2 22 ♔f1 ♘b4 23 ♕e3 e5!

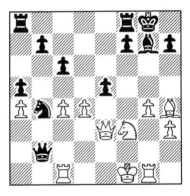

As with 10...d5 Black strives to open the position even at the cost of a pawn. With White's king being so exposed this has to be the right thing to do.

24 ♘xe5?

On 24 dxe5 Black can play 24...♘d3: for example, 25 ♖d1 ♘xe5 26 ♘xe5 ♖ae8 27 ♖g2 ♕b4 28 ♖d7 ♖xe5 recovering the piece with an extra pawn.

24...c5

Undermining the position of White's knight on e5. There was another good line in 24...f6 25 ♘f3 ♖ae8.

25 ♖e1 cxd4 26 ♕f2 ♕xf2+ 27 ♗xf2 ♖ac8 28 ♖g3 ♖fe8 29 ♘d3

29 ♗xd4? loses on the spot to 29...♘c2.

29...♖xe1+ 30 ♗xe1 ♘c2 31 ♗xa5 ♘e3+ 32 ♖xe3?!

This makes the job easier.

32...dxe3 33 c5 ♖a8 34 ♗b6 ♖xa4 35 ♔e2 ♗d4 36 ♘f4 ♗xc5 37 ♗xc5 ♖xf4 38 ♗xe3 ♖e4 0-1

30) Castle with care

"A player, wishful not to disclose his plans too soon in order not to facilitate his adversary's decision, will not infrequently preserve for himself the option of castling on either side, so as to be able to make his decision at the last possible moment. We can say at once that an attacking player will be even inclined to castle on the opposite side to that chosen by his opponent in order to bring about, by this stratagem, a more lively contest."

Savielly Tartakower (*A Breviary of Chess*)

Another old rule that is often hard-wired into players is that of 'castling early'. Whilst it is indeed often a good idea to castle early there are many exceptions, and indeed Tartakower's advice about keeping options open deserves careful consideration.

This idea can also be extended to a player's entire game in that it's often good to look for moves which contain multiple ideas. This can make life much more difficult for an opponent than secular planning as he is forced to consider every eventuality.

The following game is a good example of natural but dubious castling by Black. White sets up a pawn wedge with e4-e5 and sets about dominating the kingside dark squares. Had Black delayed castling he would have been able to undermine the e5-pawn with ...h7-h6 and ...g6-g5.

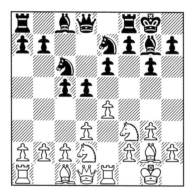

Game 38
V.Ciocaltea-N.Illijin
Romanian Championship,
Timisoara 1976
King's Indian Attack

1 e4 c5 2 ♘f3 e6 3 d3 d5 4 ♘bd2 ♘c6 5 g3 g6 6 ♗g2 ♗g7 7 0-0 ♘ge7 8 ♖e1 0-0?!

This looks like the most natural move on the board but, perhaps surprisingly, it is in fact quite a serious mistake.

In the later game L.Ljubojevic-G.Kasparov, Niksic 1983, Black gave a model demonstration of how to play this position by delaying castling in-definitely: 8...b6 9 h4 (in this position 9 e5 can be met by 9...h6 10 h4 ♕c7 11 ♕e2 and now 11...g5! 12 hxg5 hxg5 13 ♘xg5 ♕xe5 with the better game for Black) 9...h6 10 c3 a5! 11 a4 ♖a7! 12 ♘b3 d4 13 cxd4 cxd4 14 ♗d2? (14 e5! was the right move here, with chances for both sides) 14...e5! 15 ♘c1?! ♗e6 16 ♖e2?! 0-0 17 ♗e1 f5 18 ♘d2 f4! and Black had the advantage on both sides of the board.

9 e5!

Now this move is very strong, set-ting up a powerful wedge on the dark squares. The point is that the advance of the g-pawn will be too risky for Black now that he has castled.

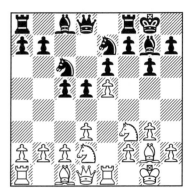

9...♕c7 10 ♕e2 b6

Black must now just live with the pawn on e5. For example after 10...h6 11 h4 g5 12 hxg5 hxg5 13 ♘xg5 ♕xe5, White can launch a devastating attack with 14 ♘de4! dxe4 15 ♕h5 ♕f5 16 ♗xe4 etc.

11 ♘f1 ♗a6 12 ♗f4 ♖ad8 13 h4 d4 14 ♘1h2

White's pieces are being brought to bear on the kingside dark squares. The e5-pawn that makes all this possible.

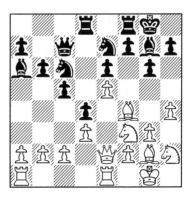

14...♘b4 15 ♕d2! ♖fe8 16 ♘g4 ♘ed5 17 ♗h6 ♗h8 18 ♗g5 ♖d7 19 a3 ♘c6 20 ♗f6! ♘xf6

On 20...h5 there would follow 21 ♘h6+! ♔h7 22 ♘g5+ ♔xh6 23 ♘xf7+ ♔h7 24 ♕h6+ ♔g8 25 ♕xh8+ ♔xf7 26 ♕g7 mate, whilst 20...♗xf6 21 exf6 ♕d8 is refuted by 22 ♘g5 ♘xf6 23 ♘xf6+ ♕xf6 24 ♗xc6 winning a whole rook.

21 exf6 h5

After 21...♕d8 White wins with 22 ♕h6! ♗xf6 23 ♘g5!.

22 ♘h6+! ♔f8 23 ♘g5 ♗xf6 24 ♘h7+ ♔g7 25 ♘xf6 ♔xf6

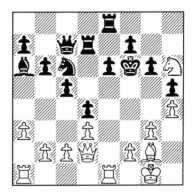

26 ♘f5!

This is a brilliant coup de grâce. Black is threatened with the move 27 ♕g5+ and has little choice but to take the knight.

26...exf5 27 ♖xe8 ♔g7 28 ♖ae1 ♘d8 29 ♕g5 c4

On 29...♘e6 White has 30 ♖1xe6 fxe6 31 ♖xe6, and 29...f6 is refuted by 30 ♖g8+!.

30 ♖h8! ♘e6

Or 30...♔xh8 31 ♕h6+ ♔g8 32 ♖e8 mate.

31 ♕h6+ ♔f6 32 ♖e8! 1-0

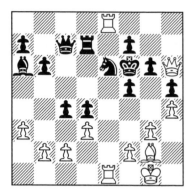

There's no good defence to the threat of 33 ♕h8+ ♘g7 34 ♖g8.

Chapter Four

The Middlegame

"In quietness you are like a maiden, in motion you are like a dragon. The mountains seem to fly when you apply our mind, the seas overflow when you apply your power."
Wang Xiang Zhai (founder of Yiquan)

The middlegame is the hardest part of chess to categorize because of its richness and variety. The number of themes and strategies is far greater than in the endgame. Unlike the opening it cannot be pinned down as variations arising from the initial position.

This makes it difficult to write about, which in turn explains why there are so few good books on the middlegame. This makes it difficult for amateurs with limited time to study, and most strong players gain their expertise from lengthy dedication to the art and extensive tournament experience.

For these reasons this section was especially challenging; how does one come up with a mere 10 rules to guide someone's footsteps in this extensive terrain? The ones I finally decided upon will hopefully address some of the flaws and misunderstandings I've seen at amateur level and seed thoughts that will lead to further growth. This process will not be quick or easy, as lessons in chess have to be learned and relearned.

31) Recognize patterns

"Those who cannot learn from history are doomed to repeat it."

George Santayana

"One of the outstanding qualities of a modern Grandmaster is his 'pattern'-knowledge, i.e. the reconnaissance of an enormous amount of typical middle/endgame structures. He 'understands' the problems concerning those pawn structures and strives to produce such positions.

"A striking example is Karpov's handling of the Black pieces: Against: 1 e4 he plays 1...c5 2 ♘f3 e6 3 d4 cxd4 4 ♘xd4 and then goes for the so-called Paulsen set-up. 1 d4 he plays 1...♘f6 2 c4 e6 and then the Nimzo or the Queen's Indian according to circumstances. 1 c4 he plays 1...e6 or 1...c5, striving for the same type of pawn-structure.

"The same attitude is to be found with other Grandmasters, e.g. Andersson, Ljubojevic. There is no reason to believe that these structures are 'better' than other structures – they produce a slightly cramped game, but a solid centre, something to work with – provided you are convinced about your superior technique & patience.

"The ZOOM 001 is a course in pattern-recognition for the Grünfeld-structure, playing the model as Black or White – you will always find yourself in a special 'family of structures' making it infinitely more easy to find a reasonable plan of campaign.

"ZOOM 001 is a modern method of moulding a & b & c into a logical, universal system of how to play chess.

"ZOOM 001 constitutes a complete language for playing/discussing chess – a model in the sense of creating a masterfile for the flow of your ideas – and how to handle the problems in practical over-the-board play."

Stephan Zeuthen (*ZOOM 001: Zero Hour for Operative Opening Models*)

ZOOM 001 is one of my favourite books because it is the only one I know of which explicitly states that a large part of chess is pattern recognition. Research by cognitive scientists into the process of chess mastery has confirmed this view, so it is the duty of every aspiring player to invest heavily in a pattern bank.

During my teenage years I spent time going over hundreds of master games, my favourite medium being the games collections of great players. This proved to be invaluable in building up my pattern bank, though at the time I just did it for fun.

Early in a game chess patterns will often repeat themselves according to the opening that was employed, which is why playing through complete games with a particular opening will help someone play that opening well. There are also many chess patterns which are independent of the opening played, the following being an example from one of my own recent games.

Game 39
N.Davies-D.James
Liverpool League 2009

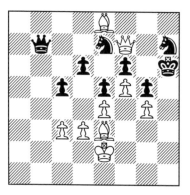

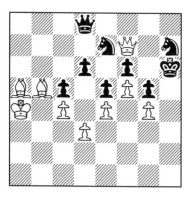

In this position Black is completely tied up, but it is not easy to administer the coup de grâce. I found the winning plan when a game I had seen over a quarter of a century earlier popped into my head.

43 ♗d2 ♛a7 44 ♗b5 ♛c7 45 ♔d1 ♛d8 46 ♗e8

Preventing 46...♛f8.

46...♛c7 47 ♔c2 ♛d8 48 c4 ♛c7 49 ♔b3!

White's plan finally becomes clear: he is going to get his king through on the queenside. This kind of thing is quite common in the endgame but with the queens on the board it is far less usual.

49...♛b7+ 50 ♗b5 ♛a7 51 ♗c3 ♛c7 52 ♔a4 ♛d8 53 ♗a5

With White's king at the gates of the enemy citadel, the exchange of queens produces an easily winning endgame.

53...♛f8 54 ♛xf8+ ♘xf8 55 ♗d8 1-0

After 55...♘g8 White has a range of winning moves including 56 ♗c7 and 56 ♗e8.

Below is the game which inspired me to attack with my king against James, a brilliant performance by the former Soviet Champion, Lev Psakhis. I remembered this game well because it was played in the critical England-USSR encounter in the 1983 World Student Team Championships.

Game 40
L.Psakhis-M.Hebden
World Student Team Ch.,
Chicago 1983
Ruy Lopez

1 e4 e5 2 ♘f3 ♘c6 3 ♗b5 a6 4 ♗a4 ♘f6

5 0-0 ♗e7 6 ♖e1 b5 7 ♗b3 0-0 8 a4 ♗b7 9 d3 d6 10 ♘c3 ♘a5 11 ♗a2 b4 12 ♘e2 c5 13 c3 c4 14 ♘g3 cxd3 15 ♕xd3 b3 16 ♗b1 ♖e8 17 ♘f5 ♗f8 18 ♗g5 h6 19 ♗xf6 ♕xf6 20 ♘e3 ♕d8 21 ♘d2 ♗c6 22 ♘d5 ♗e7 23 ♖a3 ♗g5 24 ♘xb3 ♘xb3 25 ♖xb3 ♗xa4 26 ♖b6 ♖b8 27 ♕xa6 ♖xb6 28 ♘xb6 ♗c6 29 ♗a2 ♕c7 30 ♘d5 ♗xd5 31 ♗xd5 ♖b8 32 ♕e2 ♗d8 33 g3 ♕e7 34 h4 ♗b6 35 ♖d1 ♗a7 36 b4 ♕c7 37 ♖d3 g6 38 ♕g4 ♔g7 39 ♖f3 ♖f8 40 h5 g5 41 ♕f5 ♕e7 42 ♔g2

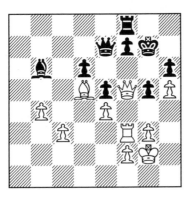

43 ♔f1!

Commencing the long march to the queenside after which White's king provides the last ingredient that finally pushes Black's defensive resources beyond breaking point. This is only possible because Black is so tied down to the defence of his f7-pawn.

43...♗a7 44 ♔e2 ♗b6 45 ♔d3 ♗a7 46 ♔c4 ♕c7+ 47 ♔b3 ♕e7 48 g4!

Getting pawns off dark squares in preparation for the possibility of an opposite-coloured bishop endgame.

48...♗b6 49 ♔c4 ♗a7 50 ♔b5! ♕e8+

After 50...♖b8+ White can play 51 ♔a6!! when 51...♖b6+ (51...♖f8 52 ♕xf7+

♖xf7 53 ♖xf7+ ♕xf7 54 ♗xf7 ♗xf2 shows the point behind White's 48 g4) 52 ♔a5 leaves Black without any useful checks and unable to defend the f7-pawn.

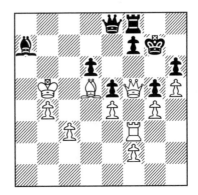

51 ♗c6!

And not 51 ♔a6?? because of 51...♕a4+ 52 ♔b7 ♖b8+ 53 ♔c7 ♗b6+ 54 ♔xb8 ♕a7+ 55 ♔c8 ♕c7 mate.

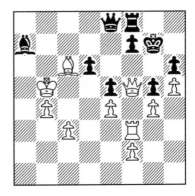

51...♕d8!

51...♕e7 52 ♕d7 would immediately clarify matters in White's favour.

52 ♔c4! ♕e7 53 ♕d7 ♕e6+! 54 ♕xe6 fxe6 55 ♖xf8 ♔xf8 56 ♔b5

This opposite-coloured bishop endgame is winning for White but it still requires some work and accuracy.

56...♔e7 57 ♔a6 ♗xf2 58 c4 ♔d8 59 ♔b7 ♗e1 60 b5 ♗f2 61 b6 ♗d4 62 ♗a4

(see following diagram)

62...d5

On 62...♗e3 White has 63 ♔c6 ♔c8 (or 63...♗c5 64 b7) 64 ♔xd6 ♗xb6 65 ♔xe5 winning the e6-pawn as well, while if 62...♗c5 White plays 63 ♗b5! ♗e3 64 ♔c6 with similar variations.

63 cxd5 exd5 64 exd5 e4 65 ♔c6! ♔c8 66 d6 e3 67 ♗b5 ♗f6 68 ♗a6+ ♔b8 69

♔d7 1-0

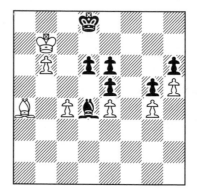

32) Think in terms of 'pawn islands'

"We have examined factors such as backward and isolated pawns and been delighted by defended pawns, especially when they are passed. However, there are factors which take account of pawn formation as a whole, and often prove decisive in defining who has the advantage or can even count on a certain win.

"Once upon a time supporters of the Steinitz-Tarrasch school had a very high opinion of a queenside pawn majority. If, for example, White had three sound pawns on the queenside opposed by only two black pawns then this was considered to be not far short of a clear win. Modern strategy on the other hand categorically denies that such a majority is an independent factor of any importance. It confidently states that it is an unwarranted assumption to claim that a wing pawn majority, taken by itself independent of the piece set up, is an advantage.

"Practical play has increasingly confirmed the new assessment and attention has been given instead to the concept of 'Pawn Islands'. Let us examine this.

"If you have all seven or eight pawns linked in a single chain whereas your opponent's pawns are split into several isolated detachments (or 'little islands' as Capablanca called them), then you have a real advantage whose benefits you will feel more and more as the game approaches the endgame stage. This apparently abstract concept has now assumed considerable importance in assessing positions."

Alexander Kotov (*Think Like a Grandmaster*)

In my view this is one of the most useful ways of looking at pawn structure and should really override the old fashioned counting of individual pawn weaknesses. A player can have several sets of doubled pawns but these can nonetheless provide cover for important squares. Counting 'pawn islands' provides a far broader and more holistic view of the structure; to my knowledge the best positional players think more in these terms.

One of the most subtle positional players in chess history is Anatoly Karpov but his games can be difficult to understand. One of the keys is the 'pawn island' concept and you can see many examples of him outplaying his opponents due to a deeper understanding of the pawn structure. Time after time he gets fewer pawn islands than his opponents and then squeezes them to death in the endgame.

The following encounter is a beautiful example, with Karpov apparently doing very little early on except getting two pawn islands against his opponent's three. But as the game progresses the strength of White's position becomes increasingly apparent until he wins a famous victory in the endgame.

Game 41
A.Karpov-A.Sokolov
Candidates Final
(10th game), Linares 1987
Queen's Indian Defence

1 d4 ♘f6 2 c4 e6 3 ♘f3 b6 4 g3 ♗a6 5 b3 ♗b4+ 6 ♗d2 ♗e7 7 ♘c3 0-0 8 e4 d5 9 cxd5 ♗xf1 10 ♔xf1

White's loss of castling rights is not too important because by bringing his king to g2 he can castle by hand.

10...exd5 11 e5 ♘e4 12 ♕e2 ♘xc3 13 ♗xc3 ♕d7 14 ♔g2 ♘c6 15 ♖he1 ♘d8

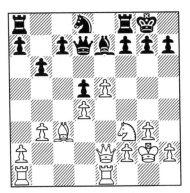

16 ♘g1!

An instructive move, preparing to mobilize his huge pawn island that stretches from d4 to h2. In order to gain some sort of counterplay Black plays for ...c7-c5, but this has the problem of leaving him with three pawn islands against White's two when he later captures on d4.

16...c5

Not 16...♘e6 17 f4 f5? because of 18 exf6 ♖xf6 19 f5! and White wins a piece.

17 f4 cxd4 18 ♗xd4 ♕f5 19 ♖ad1 ♗b4 20 ♖f1 ♘e6

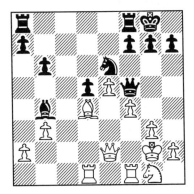

21 ♕d3!

Typical Karpov. Black's temporary activity is best snuffed out by the exchange of queens after which his structural inferiority will make itself felt.

21...♕xd3 22 ♖xd3 ♖ac8 23 ♘f3 ♖c2+ 24 ♖f2 ♖fc8

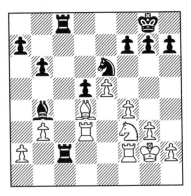

25 f5

The island advances as a single, powerful unit.

25...♘xd4 26 ♘xd4 ♖xf2+ 27 ♔xf2 ♖c1 28 g4 ♔f8 29 ♔f3 ♖f1+ 30 ♔g3 ♖c1 31 ♔f4 h6 32 h4 ♔e8 33 ♘f3 ♖c2 34 a4 ♖b2 35 ♘d4 ♗e7 36 h5

Another interesting possibility was 36 g5!? intending f5-f6.

36...a6 37 ♔f3! ♗c5 38 ♘e2 d4

The pawn had little choice but to advance but in doing so it blocks in Black's dark-squared bishop and gives the e4-square to White's king.

39 ♘f4 ♔d7 40 e6+ ♔e8

After 40...fxe6 41 ♘xe6 Black would be unable to defend g7.

41 ♔e4 a5 42 ♖f3! ♖b1 43 ♘d5!

43...♖g1?

Allowing White's king to penetrate on the queenside.

Black's best was 43...♔f8! 44 e7+! ♗xe7 45 ♔xd4 ♖g1 when White would play 46 ♔c4!! ♖xg4+ 47 ♔b5 going after Black's queenside pawns. Even so, this would be far from easy for White to win.

44 ♔d3! ♖xg4 45 f6! ♗d6

Black probably missed 45 f6! when he went hunting the g4-pawn. After 45...fxe6 there would follow 46 f7+ ♔d7 (46...♔f8 47 ♘c7 wins immediately) 47 ♘xb6+ ♔c6 48 ♘c4 intending ♘c4-e5-g6 and White wins.

46 ♘xb6! ♖g5 47 fxg7 ♖xg7 48 ♘c4 ♗b4 49 exf7+ ♖xf7 50 ♖xf7 ♔xf7 51 ♘e5+ ♔f6 52 ♘c6 ♗e1 53 ♘xd4 ♗b4

53...♔g5 54 ♘f3+ wins the bishop.

54 ♘c6 ♗e1 55 ♔e2 ♗c3 56 ♔d3 ♗e1 57 ♔c4 ♔g5

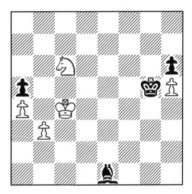

58 ♘xa5

This knight sacrifice is decisive, as the bishop is unable to cope with White's two passed pawns supported by the king.

♗xa5 59 b4 ♗d8 60 a5 ♔xh5 61 ♔b5 ♗g5 62 a6 ♗e3 63 ♔c6 1-0

63...♔g5 64 b5 h5 65 b6 would see White queen first.

33) Improve your worst-placed piece

"The fact that a single badly placed piece can cause the loss of the game can be seen in a large number of games played both in this century and the last. Tarrasch has the memorable phrase, 'If one piece stands badly the whole position is bad'."

Alexander Kotov (*Think Like a Grandmaster*)

In my own practice I've often had to fight against lines of the King's Indian Defence in which a black knight goes to a5, for example in the line 1 d4 ♘f6 2 c4 g6 3 ♘f3 ♗g7 4 g3 0-0 5 ♗g2 d6 6 0-0 ♘c6 7 ♘c3 a6 8 d5 ♘a5 9 ♘d2 c5. Is Black's knight on a5 an asset or a liability? Theoreticians are divided on the matter, though Black must certainly get counterplay against c4 if he is to justify its placement.

In the following game Black got into the same kind of position but lost time with ...♗c8-g4 and then later retreating his bishop to d7. This is all that is needed to turn a controversial issue into a very one-sided one and I managed to win quite easily.

Game 42
N.Davies-F.Rayner
Wrexham 1994
King's Indian Defence

1 d4 ♘f6 2 ♘f3 g6 3 c4 ♗g7 4 g3 0-0 5 ♗g2 c5 6 0-0 d6 7 b3 ♘c6 8 ♗b2

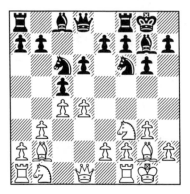

8...♗g4?!

This invites White's d-pawn to push on to d5 in a situation in which Black's queen's bishop is not at all well placed on g4.

Black has several superior possibilities:

a) 8...♘e4 is the traditional choice in this line, though maybe White can eke out an edge with 9 ♘bd2!? (9 e3 ♗g4 10 ♕c1 ♗xf3 11 ♗xf3 ♘g5 12 ♗xc6 bxc6 13 dxc5 dxc5 14 ♗xg7 ♔xg7 15 f4 ♘e4 16 ♘c3 ♕d3 17 ♘xe4 ♕xe4 18 ♕c3+ ♔g8 did not leave White with much in V.Korchnoi-S.Gligoric, Belgrade 1956) 9...♗f5 10 ♘h4!?. For example, 10...♘xd2 11 ♕xd2 ♘xd4 12 ♘xf5 ♘xf5 13 ♗xg7 ♘xg7 14 ♗xb7 ♖b8 15 ♗f3 ♕c7 16 h4 h5 17 ♖ac1 ♔h7 18 ♖c3 ♕d7 19 ♖d3 gave White some chances in O.Romanishin-T.Halasz, Gyor 1990.

b) 8...cxd4 9 ♘xd4 ♗d7 10 ♘c3 ♕a5 11 e3 ♖ab8 12 ♖e1 ♖fc8 13 h3 a6 14 a3 ♕d8 15 ♖c1 ♘a5 16 ♘d5 was a bit better for White in O.Romanishin-B.Gulko, USSR Championship, Tbilisi 1978.

9 d5 ♘a5 10 ♘c3 a6 11 ♘d2 ♖b8 12 ♕c2 b5 13 h3 ♗d7 14 ♖ab1 bxc4 15 bxc4

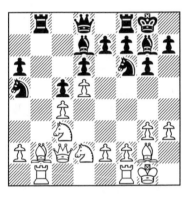

In this kind of position the battle revolves around Black's knight on a5. Even though the knight puts some pressure on c4 its only hope in life is to be able to capture this pawn. If it does not manage to do that then its prospects are grim indeed. For example, a retreat to b7 and d8 will still leave it stymied by White's pawn on d5.

15...♗h6 16 f4 e5 17 dxe6 ♗xe6 18 ♘d5 ♗xd5 19 cxd5

This does not do much for the prospects of the knight on a5. Now it does not even have the c4-pawn to target.

19...♗g7

After 19...♘h5 20 ♔h2 ♕c7 White can play 21 ♘e4: for example, 21...f5 22 ♘xd6! ♖xb2 (22...♕xd6 23 ♗e5 wins immediately) 23 ♕xb2 ♕xd6 24 ♕c3

♕d8 (24...♘xg3 25 ♔xg3 ♗xf4+ 26 ♖xf4 g5 27 e3 is not much better) and now 25 d6! highlights the plight of the a5-knight.

20 ♔h2 c4 21 ♗c3 ♕c7 22 e4 ♕c5?!

22...♘d7 would be more tenacious, but this is still great for White after 23 ♗xg7 ♔xg7 24 ♕c3+ f6 (if 24...♔g8 White can play 25 e5 dxe5 26 d6) 25 ♘f3 followed by 26 ♘d4.

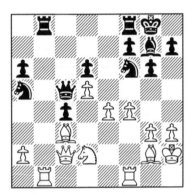

23 ♗xf6! ♗xf6

Or if 23...♖xb1 24 ♖xb1 ♗xf6 then 25 e5 ♗e7 26 ♘e4 ♕a3 27 ♖b6! is very strong.

24 e5 ♗e7 25 ♘e4 ♕a3?

Losing immediately, though it is difficult to give Black good advice here. For example, 25...♕a7 is strongly met by 26 ♕a4 ♘b7 (26...♖xb1 27 ♖xb1 ♘b7 28 ♕d7 is even worse) 27 ♕d7 ♖fe8 28 exd6 etc.

26 ♖f3 1-0

Black's queen has nowhere to go.

So if a badly placed piece can spell doom, what should someone do to avoid such a predicament? I have an expression that I like to use for moves that improve bad pieces, which is 'gardening moves'. Certainly at club level there tends to be a paucity of such moves, players preferring to chase apparent opportunities with the pieces already in play.

In the following example Lasker gives us a brilliant demonstration of how to improve the worst-placed piece. His move 22 ♘b1 starts the process of bringing his knight to a better square and steps up the pressure on Pillsbury's position.

Game 43
E.Lasker-H.Pillsbury
Paris 1900
Dutch Defence

---

1 d4 f5 2 e4 fxe4 3 ♘c3 ♘f6 4 ♗g5 c6 5 f3 exf3 6 ♘xf3 e6 7 ♗d3 ♗e7 8 ♘e5 0-0 9 ♗xf6 ♖xf6 10 ♕h5 g6 11 ♘xg6 ♕e8 12 ♘xe7+ ♕xe7 13 0-0-0 d5 14 ♖de1 ♘d7 15 ♖e3 ♖f7 16 ♖g3+ ♔h8 17 ♗g6 ♖g7 18 ♖f1 ♘f6 19 ♕h4 ♘g8 20 ♕xe7 ♖xe7 21 ♗d3 ♗d7

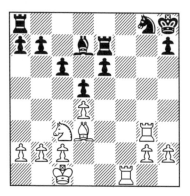

In this position the only white piece

that is not participating is his knight on c3. Accordingly Lasker sets about improving it.

22 ♘b1!

A very instructive move. The knight is setting off for the e5-square via d2 and f3.

22...♖ae8

Getting rid of the e5 weakness with 22...e5?! is not good because of 23 dxe5 ♖xe5? 24 ♖f7 ♖e7 25 ♖xg8+ etc.

23 ♘d2 e5

Otherwise White will play 24 ♘f3.

24 dxe5 ♖xe5 25 ♘f3 ♖e3

Or if 25...♖5e7 there follows 26 ♘g5 ♗e6 27 ♔d2, leaving Black completely tied up.

26 ♘g5

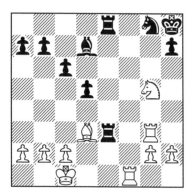

Five moves ago, this knight was doing nothing; now it is threatening mate in one.

26...♖xg3 27 hxg3 h6

After 27...♖e7 White can just play 28 ♘xh7! because after 28...♖xh7 29 ♗xh7 ♔xh7 White has 30 ♖f7+ winning the bishop on d7.

28 ♘f7+ ♔g7 29 ♘d6 ♖e7 30 ♘xb7

Winning a pawn. Although the extra pawn is currently doubled, for an endgame player of Lasker's class it proves to be a decisive factor.

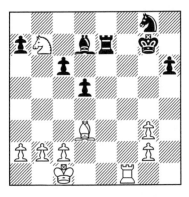

30...♘f6 31 ♘c5 ♗g4 32 ♖f4 ♗c8 33 ♖a4 ♘g4 34 ♗a6 ♗f5 35 ♖f4 ♘e3 36 c3 ♔g6 37 ♖f2 ♗e4 38 b3 ♗xg2 39 ♗d3+ ♔g5 40 ♖f8 ♔g4 41 ♖g8+ ♔f3 42 ♖g6

Lasker has found the right way to win: exchanging the pawns on the kingside and then attacking Black's queenside weaknesses with everything that he has.

42...♘g4 43 ♗f5 h5 44 ♖g5 ♖e1+ 45 ♔b2 ♖h1 46 ♗g6 ♔xg3 47 ♗xh5 ♗f3 48 ♗xg4 ♗xg4 49 ♖g6 ♖h2+ 50 ♔a3 ♖c2 51 ♘d3!

And not 51 ♖xc6 because of 51...♖xc3 52 ♘e4+ dxe4 53 ♖xc3+ ♔f2

with a powerful passed e-pawn that must be reckoned with.

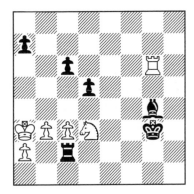

51...♔h4 52 ♘e5 ♗f5 53 ♖xc6 ♔g3 54 ♖c5 ♖d2 55 ♘c6 ♔f4 56 ♘b4 d4 57 cxd4 ♖xd4 58 ♖a5 ♖d7 59 ♘c6 ♗e4 60 ♘xa7

Finally it's clear that White is winning, though Pillsbury keeps fighting for another 25 moves.

60...♖d1 61 ♘b5 ♖d5 62 ♔b4 ♗d3 63 ♘c7 ♖xa5 64 ♔xa5 ♔e5 65 ♔b4 ♔d6 66 ♘b5+ ♔c6 67 a4 ♔b6 68 ♘a3 ♗e2 69 ♘c4+ ♔a6 70 ♔c3 ♗d1 71 ♘b2 ♗h5 72 b4 ♗e8 73 ♔b3 ♗c6 74 ♔c4 ♗d7 75 ♔c5 ♗g4 76 ♘c4 ♗d1 77 b5+ ♔a7 78 a5 ♗f3 79 ♘e5 ♗b7 80 ♘c6+ ♔a8 81 ♔b6 ♗a6 82 ♘b4 ♗b7 83 ♘a6 ♗f3 84 ♘c7+ ♔b8 85 a6 1-0

34) Harmonize your bishops and pawns

An important property of bishops is that they only cover squares of a particular colour. This means that if a player has only one of his bishops left, a certain weakness can easily appear on the squares that it does not cover.

Generally speaking this means that with one bishop left it is better to try and put pawns on the *opposite* colour to that bishop so as not to leave weaknesses. Of course there are sometimes more urgent priorities than neatly arranging bishops and pawns in complementary fashion but it should always be kept in mind. In strong Grandmasters this awareness reaches an instinctive level so these days it is very rare that someone manages to win a high-level game based purely on an opponent's bad bishop.

This is what makes the following game so remarkable; it is a 'bad bishop' game won against one of the most subtle positional players in chess history, Ulf Andersson.

Game 44
A.Miles-U.Andersson
Las Palmas 1980
Réti Opening

---

1 g3 c5 2 ♗g2 ♘c6 3 ♘f3 g6 4 c3 ♗g7 5 d4 cxd4 6 cxd4 d5 7 ♘c3 e6!?

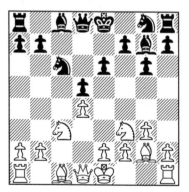

An interesting break in the symmetry. The usual move is 7...♘f6 after which 8 0-0 0-0 9 ♘e5 is well charted territory.

8 ♗f4 ♘ge7 9 ♕d2!?

The start of an interesting plan by Miles to exchange off the bishop which harmonizes with Black's pawns, i.e. the one on g7.

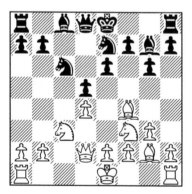

9...0-0

There is a case for delaying castling with 9...♘f5. A.Miles-G.Sosonko, Tilburg 1981, continued 10 ♘b5 0-0 11 g4 ♘fe7 12 h3 ♗d7 13 0-0 a6 14 ♘c3 ♖c8 with a position that was starting to look very equal.

10 ♗h6 ♗xh6 11 ♕xh6 ♘f5 12 ♕d2 b6

Perhaps Black should play 12...♕b6 after which 13 e3 will stop White's queen from going to h6 any time soon.

13 ♖d1 ♗a6 14 h4 ♘a5?

After this White gets a strong initiative on the kingside.

Although 14...h5 would be well met by 15 ♕f4 intending ♗g2-h3 and g3-g4, there were more promising alternatives for Black in 14...f6, 14...♖c8 and 14...♕f6.

15 g4

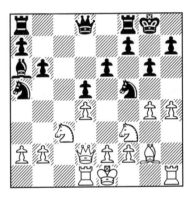

15...♘d6

After 15...♘c4 White can play 16 ♕c1, when 16...♘fd6 17 b3 ♘a5 18 h5 ♖c8 19 hxg6 fxg6 20 ♕e3 gives him a clear advantage.

16 h5 ♕f6 17 hxg6 fxg6

Opening the h-file with 17...hxg6 would be fatal for Black after 18 g5!

♕e7 (18...♕g7 19 ♕f4 followed by ♘f3-e5-g4 would be equally unpleasant) 19 ♕f4 (threatening 20 ♕h2) 19...♔g7 20 ♕e5+ f6 21 gxf6+ ♖xf6 22 ♘xd5 and White wins.

18 ♕h6 ♖f7

On 18...♕f7 White should protect the f2-pawn with 19 ♕h4 whereupon he is threatening 20 ♘g5.

19 g5! ♕g7

After 19...♕e7 20 ♘e5 ♖g7 White can even play 21 ♗xd5!.

20 ♘e5

20...♕xh6

So at least Black manages to avoid losing in the middlegame, but the endgame is none too pleasant either. He has a classic 'bad bishop' disadvantage in which the light-squared bishop on a6 does not harmonize with his light-squared pawns at all.

21 ♖xh6 ♖ff8

Black still has to watch out for tactics, for example 21...♖e7 22 ♘xd5!.

22 ♘d7 ♖f7 23 ♘f6+ ♔h8 24 ♗h3! ♗c8

On 24...♘f5 there follows 25 ♗xf5 gxf5 26 ♔d2 (intending 27 ♖dh1) 26...♘c4+ 27 ♔c1 ♖c8 (27...♖b8 28 ♖dh1 ♖bb7 29 ♘h5 is also winning) 28 ♖dh1 ♖cc7 29 ♘e8! threatening both g5-g6 and ♘e8-♘f6.

25 ♔d2!

Once again preparing to bring the rook on d1 to h1.

25...♖g7 26 f4 ♖b8 27 ♖h1 ♘ac4+ 28 ♔d3 ♖bb7

28...♘xb2+? 29 ♔c2 ♘bc4 30 ♗xe6! wins for White.

29 b3 ♘a3 30 e4! dxe4+ 31 ♘cxe4 ♘xe4

After 31...♘ab5 there might follow 32 a4 ♘xe4 33 ♘xe4 ♘c7 34 ♘f6 ♘a6 35 d5 ♘c5+ 36 ♔c2 with a winning position.

32 ♔xe4 ♘b5

Or if 32...♖bc7 then 33 ♔e5! ♗b7 34 ♖h2 ♖c1 35 ♗f5 ♖e1+ 36 ♗e4 is winning.

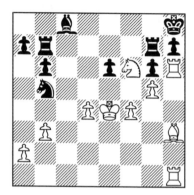

33 ♔e5!

Threatening d4-d5.

33...♖be7 34 ♗f1! 1-0

When Black moves his knight from b5, White can play the deadly 35 ♗d3. This was an amazing achievement by Miles when you consider who his opponent was.

35) Keep the tension

Years ago, during one of my games with Nigel Short, I made a superficially active but weakening move which almost cost me the game. Afterwards Nigel quizzed me as to why I played this way to which I replied that "I'm a busy kind of player". "Yes," replied the other Nigel, "even when there's nothing to do."

Knowing that you can learn a lot from the insights of great players I took Nigel's words quite seriously. Reviewing some of my games I realized that he was quite right; I did have a definite tendency to try to do things even when there was nothing to do. As soon as tension appeared in the position I found it difficult to resist the opportunity to play some 'forcing moves' no matter where they led.

Since then I have come to realize that one of the hallmarks of very strong players is the ability to recognize when they should try to do something and when it is better to play a move which just simply improves their position. This is why top-class games often give the impression that nothing is really happening whereas in reality their outwardly innocuous moves represent a cagey struggle to outmanoeuvre their opponent. The two adversaries are working towards the right moment to strike, knowing full well that a premature attempt to force matters could simply lose the advantage or even totally rebound.

Almost all players start out by playing a brand of forceful tactical chess which is the clearest and simplest route to success. As we improve and come up against ever stronger opposition we all gradually realize that tactics alone are not enough. In fact there will inevitably come a point at which it is necessary to think strategically in order to enjoy continued success.

Club-level players can't usually afford the luxury of spending unlimited time with which to perfect their chess, so as chess players they often remain youthful tacticians. There is a tendency to indulge in forcing moves regardless of whether they are good or bad, and any tension between pieces and pawns is resolved very quickly.

There is no easy cure for this tendency; the only one that really works is to spend years studying and playing chess after which greater insight gradually develops. Having said that, I can point out one or two of the most common scenarios in which the tension is usually resolved prematurely. Hopefully you will be able to avoid these mistakes yourself and even lure your opponents into making them. You just need to get them into the right kind of position.

The following two snippets from games by one of my students show a classic tension-releasing mistake in the Torre Attack, Black playing ...c5-c4. The problem is that this takes the pressure off the d4-pawn and enables White to play e3-e4 without any problems. But to many players' eyes it looks like it gains time and space.

Game 45
B.Carty-M.Connelly
Dublin League 1996
Torre Attack

1 d4 d5 2 ♘f3 ♘f6 3 ♗g5 e6

With this move order Black can play 3...♘e4, and this may well be his best move here.

4 ♘bd2 ♗e7 5 e3 0-0 6 ♗d3 c5 7 c3 ♘c6 8 0-0

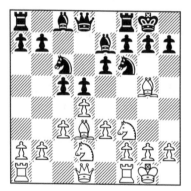

8...c4?

Nine times out of ten this is the wrong idea. In addition to making it easier for White to play e3-e4, the c4-pawn can easily become a weakness.

Black should play 8...b6, although White then has some attacking chances after 9 ♘e5.

9 ♗c2 b5 10 ♕e2 a5 11 e4 ♖e8

On 11...dxe4 there would follow 12 ♗xf6 exf3 (12...♗xf6 13 ♕xe4 forks c6

and h7) 13 ♕e4 g6 14 ♗xe7 winning a piece.

12 e5 ♘d7 13 ♗xe7 ♕xe7 14 ♘e4!

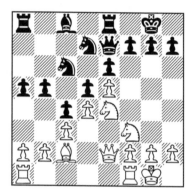

Very nice play by White. After 14...dxe4 15 ♕xe4 White wins a pawn because of the simultaneous attack on c6 and h7.

14...f6 15 ♘d6

White enjoys a clear advantage and went on to win in 33 moves.

Game 46
B.Carty-Hearns
Dublin League 1997
Torre Attack

1 d4 ♘f6 2 ♘f3 e6 3 ♗g5 ♗e7 4 ♘bd2 d5 5 e3 ♘bd7 6 ♗d3 0-0

There's a school of thought which says that such early castling by Black is premature in the Torre Attack. There's a good case for first developing the queenside with 6...c5 followed by

7...b6.

7 0-0 h6 8 ♗h4 c5 9 c3 c4?

Again we see this release of tension; at club level it is very common. Black should play 9...b6.

10 ♗c2 ♛b6 11 ♖b1 ♛c7

(see following diagram)

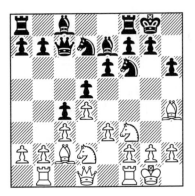

12 ♗g3

The immediate 12 e4 was also good.

12...♗d6 13 e4

and once again White had the advantage.

36) All that glitters is not gold

"A brilliant combination bewitches men to such an extent that they willingly believe falsehoods and are blinded to the truth. The criticism, which in the long run comes as irresistibly as death, has to voice its unbiased judgement."

Emanuel Lasker (*Lasker's Manual of Chess*)

In his great book, Lasker discusses aesthetics in chess quite extensively, arguing that the objective scientific values of moves were what was important rather than their apparent 'beauty'. At the time this was quite a big issue, with 'combinative' players being deemed to be playing the game in the proper spirit whilst the rational approach of Wilhelm Steinitz and then Lasker himself was somehow thought to be unsportsmanlike.

Lasker's thoughts are relevant even today as many players are still unwilling to give up on a beautiful-looking idea even if it is not the strongest. Their play will inevitably suffer as a result.

The finish to the following Chigorin-Steinitz game is a good example of this tendency. Chigorin had a simple and cast-iron win but then strangely rejected it in favour of an uncertain knight sacrifice.

seems to be more or less winning for White.

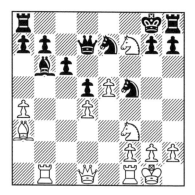

Game 47
M.Chigorin-W.Steinitz
World Championship
(1st game), Havana 1892
Evans Gambit

1 e4 e5 2 ♘f3 ♘c6 3 ♗c4 ♗c5 4 b4 ♗xb4 5 c3 ♗a5 6 0-0 d6 7 d4 ♗g4 8 ♗b5 exd4 9 cxd4 ♗d7 10 ♗b2 ♘ce7 11 ♗xd7+ ♕xd7 12 ♘a3 ♘h6 13 ♘c4 ♗b6 14 a4 c6 15 e5 d5 16 ♘d6+ ♔f8 17 ♗a3 ♔g8 18 ♖b1 ♘hf5 19 ♘xf7!?

Because of this combination this game did the rounds of the world's chess press, and indeed the sacrifice

But Lasker rightly asked whether this was really necessary when there is a simple, effective and totally convincing win to be had via 19 a5! ♗xa5 20 ♖xb7 ♗c7 21 ♘g5. Given that the point of a chess game should be the effective marshalling of one's forces to victory rather than showing off, I have to agree with Lasker's sentiment.

19...♔xf7 20 e6+ ♔xe6 21 ♘e5 ♕c8?!

Lasker tried to improve Black's defence with 21...♕e8! but this seems good for White after 22 ♖e1 ♔f6 23 ♗xe7+! ♕xe7 (23...♔xe7? 24 ♘g4+) 24 ♘g4+ ♔f7 25 ♖xe7+ ♔xe7 26 ♕e1+ etc.

If 21...♕c7 there follows 22 ♖e1 ♔f6 23 ♕f3 h5 24 ♗xe7+ ♕xe7 25 g4 g6 26 gxf5 gxf5 27 ♔h1 with an unpleasant position for Black.

22 ♖e1 ♔f6

Another defensive idea is 22...♗a5, but then White seems to have the better of it via 23 ♕h5 ♕e8 24 ♕f3 ♗xe1 25 ♖xe1 threatening 26 ♘xc6+.

23 ♕h5

Threatening mate by both ♘g4 and ♕f7.

23...g6

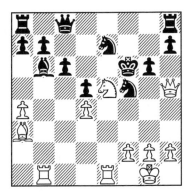

24 ♗xe7+?!

24 ♘g4+ would have been better here: for example, 24...♔f7 25 ♖xe7+ ♘xe7 26 ♘h6+ ♔g7 (or 26...♔e8 27 ♕e5) 27 ♕e5+ ♔xh6 28 ♗c1+ g5 29 ♕xg5 mate.

24...♔xe7

24...♘xe7 25 ♘g4+ ♔f7 26 ♘h6+ would be good for White, but Black could struggle on with 24...♔g7 25 ♕g5 ♖f8 26 ♗xf8+ ♕xf8. He's down the exchange but doing relatively well compared with the position he could have had after 19 a5.

25 ♘xg6+ ♔f6 26 ♘xh8 ♗xd4

Both 26...♕xh8 27 ♖e5 ♕c8 28 g4 and 26...♕d7 27 ♖b3! ♖xh8 28 ♖f3 are good for White.

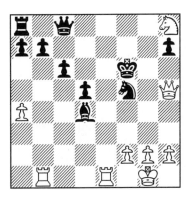

27 ♖b3 ♕d7 28 ♖f3 ♖xh8 29 g4 ♖g8 30 ♕h6+ ♖g6 31 ♖xf5+ 1-0

"Even the most lenient critic would have to say that Tschigorin fought with a corpse, gave him a new spell of life and then killed him again." – Lasker

37) Attack the weakest point

"To unfailingly take what you attack, attack where there is no defence."

Sun Tzu (*The Art of War*)

"Steinitz desires to aid the searcher. He orders the attack, but he also gives advice as to how this order can be successfully carried out. He asks which direction the attack has to take, and he answers: the target for the attack has to be a weakness in the hostile position. He therefore compares the position of your opponent to a chain of many links and yourself, the assailant, to one who wants to break the chain. He advises you to look for the point where the connection is weakest and against that to direct your efforts. Of course, if the chain offers the same resistance in every link, one cannot see a motive for selecting by chance one of these points but the chain is never equally strong in all of its links, and the master chooses after conscientious consideration, the point of least resistance as the target for his efforts."

Emanuel Lasker (*Lasker's Manual of Chess*)

This rule is important because it acts against the wilfulness that many chess players have: they choose to attack what they *want* to attack rather than what they *should* attack. A particularly noteworthy tendency is for players to play against their opponent's king almost regardless of whether it is well defended or not. Sometimes this stems from a wish to be an 'attacking' player; sometimes it is because attack is all that they know. Invariably this is a weakness.

In the following game Efim Geller, one of the greatest players in history, is seen directing his play towards Black's well-defended king. This looks very dangerous, especially because White is playing for mate. But Black carries the day by conscientiously targeting White's weaknesses on c4 and then d4.

Game 48
E.Geller-M.Euwe
Candidates Tournament,
Zürich 1953
Nimzo-Indian Defence

---

1 d4 ♘f6 2 c4 e6 3 ♘c3 ♗b4 4 e3 c5 5 a3

Known as the Sämisch, this is a sharp line in which White gains the bishop pair and tries to take the initiative on the kingside but in doing so leaves himself with doubled c-pawns.

5...♗xc3+ 6 bxc3 b6! 7 ♗d3 ♗b7

Although Black intends to bring this bishop to a6 to latch onto White's c4-pawn, he first takes the opportunity to get White to play 8 f3. This makes it slightly more difficult for White to sally forth on the kingside: for example, he cannot bring his queen directly from d1 to h5.

8 f3 ♞c6 9 ♞e2 0-0 10 0-0 ♞a5

Targeting the weakness on c4.

11 e4 ♞e8!

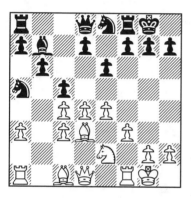

An instructive move, preventing White from pinning the knight with ♗c1-g5 and preparing to block the advance of White's f-pawn with either ...f7-f5 or ...f7-f6. Now Black prepares to attack White's weak point on c4 with ...cxd4 and ...♖c8.

12 ♞g3 cxd4 13 cxd4 ♖c8 14 f4 ♞xc4 15 f5 f6

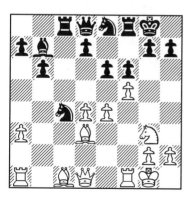

16 ♖f4

With the simple aim of bringing the rook to h4 and his queen to h5. It's not easy for Black to prevent this plan but he does have another option: counterattack!

16...b5!

Black fixes his sights on a new White weakness, the pawn on d4.

17 ♖h4 ♛b6 18 e5!

White protects the pawn on d4 whilst furthering his attacking plans on the kingside.

Euwe continues to defend himself in the most cold-blooded style, which is really what one might expect from a man who played two matches against Alexander Alekhine.

18...♞xe5 19 fxe6 ♞xd3 20 ♛xd3

And not 20 exd7 because of 20...♖xc1 21 ♖xc1 ♞xc1 etc.

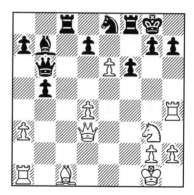

20...♛xe6

Although this move is often awarded an exclamation mark, it's not clear that it is the strongest.

20...g6? is bad because of 21 ♗h6! (and not 21 exd7? in view of 21...♛c6) 21...♞g7 22 ♗xg7 ♚xg7 23 ♞f5+! gxf5

(23...♔h8 24 ♕h3 h5 25 ♖xh5+! leads to mate) 24 ♕xf5 ♖h8 25 ♖g4+ with mate. However, 20...dxe6 21 ♕xh7+ ♔f7 looks very solid.

21 ♕xh7+ ♔f7 22 ♗h6

22 ♕h5+? does not work because of 22...g6 23 ♕h7+ (23 ♕xb5? ♗a6 wins on the spot) 23...♘g7 24 ♗h6 ♖g8 and White's attack has ground to a standstill.

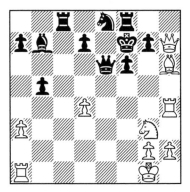

22...♖h8!?

A truly brilliant conception by Euwe which, however, may not be the best!

22...♕d5 23 ♗e4 ♖c6 intending 24...♖e6 looks good for Black, whereas now White could probably have saved himself.

23 ♕xh8 ♖c2 24 ♖c1?

Perhaps in shock after Euwe's amazing 22nd move, Geller fails to find the best defence.

He should have played 24 d5!. After 24...♗xd5 (24...♕b6+ 25 ♔h1 ♕f2 26 ♖g1 ♗xd5 27 ♖e4! ♗xe4 28 ♘xe4 ♕h4 is quite risky for Black: for example, 29 ♘d6+ ♘xd6 30 ♕xg7+ ♔e6 31 ♕g8+ ♔e5 32 ♖d1! ♕e4 33 ♗e3! gives White a winning attack) 25 ♖d1 ♖xg2+ 26 ♔f1 gxh6 27 ♕xh6! ♗f3! 28 ♖d2 Black shouldn't be in serious risk of losing, as following 28...♖xd2 29 ♕xd2 the position fizzles out into a state of relative balance.

24...♖xg2+ 25 ♔f1 ♕b3!

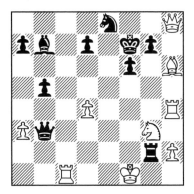

Suddenly threatening mate via ...♕f3+ or ...♕d3+. White is completely lost now.

26 ♔e1 ♕f3 0-1

White's king is getting mated.

38) In defence make every point equally weak

"Steinitz also points out the way to the defender who asks himself how to achieve this end. He advises: improve the worst weakness voluntarily. The ideal of a position for defence is that it have no linea minoris resistenciae, that all of its lines of resistance be equally strong, that the chain contain only joints of equal strength. But this ideal can never be attained. Approach it, as far as you are able! That is the test of how you do your duty as a defender. Thus, in this manner you serve your cause well, even if you lose the game."

Emanuel Lasker (*Lasker's Manual of Chess*)

The idea of presenting the opponent with no clear target is one of the most important defensive concepts which spills over to chess strategy, psychology and many modern opening systems. In the old days positions tended to be evaluated in terms of static factors such as 'space', 'time' and 'material' which has led many people to believe that these should win on their own. Lasker advocated a more dynamic understanding of these things by suggesting that a target is also required.

In the 1980s players started using a new kind of position with Black, dubbed the 'Hedgehog', which had previously been dismissed as being bad. Black sets up a cramped position in which there are also several weaknesses but argues that White will be unable to exploit any of these advantages. In many respects I consider the Hedgehog to be a child of Lasker and it naturally appealed to other original thinkers such as the Romanian Grandmaster, Mihai Suba.

Here is one of Suba's games in which he lures his opponent onto the Hedgehog's spikes.

Game 49
J.Garcia Padron-M.Suba
Las Palmas 1979
English Opening

---

1 c4 ♘f6 2 ♘c3 e6 3 ♘f3 c5 4 g3 b6 5 ♗g2 ♗b7 6 0-0 ♗e7 7 d4 cxd4 8 ♕xd4 d6 9 e4 a6 10 b3 ♘bd7 11 ♗b2 0-0 12

♖ac1 ♕b8!?

Suba explained this as 'sheer bravado'. There's nothing wrong with putting the queen on c7, but Black wants to wave a red flag at the bull.

13 ♘d2 ♖c8

The classicists would be appalled by Black's play. He has occupied just three rows and created weak pawns on d6 and b6, but White has a problem in how to get at them. For example, if he tries to attack the d6-pawn by putting his bishop on a3 and some rooks on the d-file, Black can just play his d7-knight to c5. And if White then drives the knight away with b3-b4 he weakens his c4-pawn. In a sense Black's entire position is backward but its strength is that *his weaknesses are equally weak.*

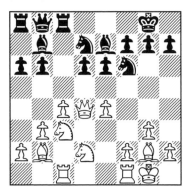

14 h3 ♗f8 15 ♖fd1 ♗c6 16 ♕e3 ♖a7 17 ♘f3 ♗a8 18 ♘d4 ♖e8 19 ♕d2 g6 20 ♔h2 ♗g7 21 ♘de2?

Attacking the pawn on d6 but releasing his grip on the b5-square. Suba takes the opportunity to strike.

21...b5! 22 cxb5 axb5

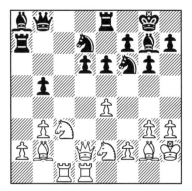

23 f3?!

23 ♕xd6 ♕xd6 24 ♖xd6 b4 would be nothing more than a trade of the d6-pawn for the one on e4. But the exchange of queens might have helped ease White's defence had he realized early enough that this was what he would have to do.

23...b4 24 ♘a4 d5 25 exd5 ♗xd5 26 ♘d4 ♖a6 27 ♕f2

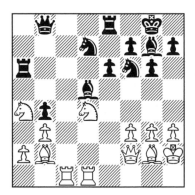

27...♘h5?

According to Suba, 27...e5! followed by 28...e4 would have been stronger.

28 f4 ♘df6 29 ♘c6 ♕b7 30 ♘e5 ♖aa8 31 ♘c5?! ♕b8 32 g4?

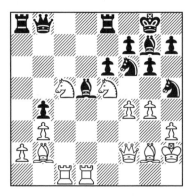

Falling into a trap. White should

have played 32 &d4 when his position would still hold together.

32...&xf4! 33 &xf4 &xa2

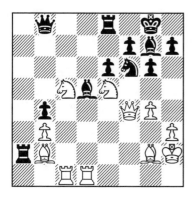

34 &c2

With his opponent in time-trouble Suba was expecting 34 &cd7 &xd7 35 &xf7+ &h8 when White can't play 36 &xg6+ followed by 37 &xg7 mate because the knight on e5 is pinned.

34...&xb2! 35 &xb2 &xg4+! 36 &xg4 &xe5+ 37 &h1 &xb2

With Black having won no less than three pawns White could really have thrown in the towel here, but he continues past the time control through inertia.

38 &xd5 exd5 39 &d7 &e2 40 &d8+ &f8 41 &b8 &c2 0-1

39) Never say die

"However hopeless the situation appears to be there yet always exists the possibility of putting up a stubborn resistance. And it is the player's task to find these opportunities and make the best of them. When the player with the upper hand is continually confronted by new problems, when, at every moment, one renders the win as difficult as possible, then it is likely that his powers will eventually weaken and he may make some mistake."

Paul Keres (*The Art of the Middle Game*)

This is one of the most useful and practical paragraphs ever written about chess from one of the most useful and practical chapters ('How to Defend Difficult Positions'). I advise most of my students to read it several times as it can instil a mentality that is invaluable for chess.

Players often seem to be under the impression that once a player has gained an advantage the conversion thereof should be a 'matter of technique'. Yet this rarely happens without at least a few hiccups, especially if one of the players adopts a 'never say die' approach.

Let's see an example from one of Keres's own games.

♗d7 34 ♕e3 ♖c8 35 ♗d3.

<table>
<tr><td>

Game 50
D.Bronstein-P.Keres
Candidates Tournament,
Amsterdam 1956
Ruy Lopez

</td></tr>
</table>

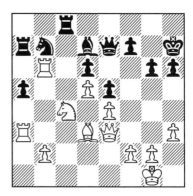

1 e4 e5 2 ♘f3 ♘c6 3 ♗b5 a6 4 ♗a4 ♘f6 5 0-0 ♗e7 6 ♖e1 b5 7 ♗b3 d6 8 c3 0-0 9 h3 ♘a5 10 ♗c2 c5 11 d4 ♕c7 12 ♘bd2 cxd4 13 cxd4 ♘c6 14 ♘b3 ♗b7 15 ♗g5 h6 16 ♗h4 ♘h5 17 d5 ♘d8 18 ♗xe7 ♕xe7 19 ♘fd4 ♘f4 20 ♘f5 ♕f6 21 ♖e3 ♔h7 22 a4 bxa4 23 ♖xa4 ♗c8 24 ♖b4 ♘b7 25 ♖c3 g6 26 ♘e3 a5 27 ♖b6 ♕d8 28 ♘c4 ♖a7 29 ♘c1 ♕g5 30 ♖g3 ♕e7 31 ♘e2 ♘xe2+ 32 ♕xe2 ♖d8 33 ♖a3

Here's what Keres wrote about this position:

"Black's plight is wretched in the extreme. White has, it is true, no plus in material, but his pieces command the whole board and it seems to be merely a matter of time before Black's position collapses. A cramped position is not in itself a disaster, but if, in addition, one has no prospects of counterplay, then the situation usually becomes quickly hopeless. This, too, is the case here. When one considers Black's plausible moves then it soon becomes apparent that he can scarcely move anything without incurring a speedy loss. The Queen and the Knight are tied to the pawn on d6; the Rook on a7 must protect the Knight, and the Bishop on d7 has only one move, to e8. One can hardly think of a more hopeless situation, but even in such a position one ought to try to find some satisfactory method of defence.

"Of course the reader will understand that I am not attempting to prove that Black's position is to be held by good defensive moves. That would be an insoluble problem, since White has a won game. Instead, the aim in this example is to demonstrate that even a position that is ripe for resignation can, despite everything, afford defensive possibilities that make the opponent's task more difficult. The game's final outcome depended less on my good defence, since in reality nothing like this is to be found, than on the psychological effect that my obstinate 'never surrender' tactics had on my opponent. These represent, however, the only kind of tactics that one can employ in such positions.

"Now, however, back to the game. What can Black try in the diagram position? Naturally, nothing. But this does not mean that he should wander planlessly to and fro, waiting to see how White will consummate his advantage for a win. In every position, no matter how bad it may be, there always exist chances for small finesses, which one must employ whenever possible. It should never be forgotten that, in a superior position, one is always looking for a clear way to win. Quite often small advantages are despised, since one wants to obtain more out of the position. This factor, easily understood from the psychological angle, must be utilized, since thereby one can often embark on variations which one would never have been wont to try in equal positions. Psychological methods of warfare are the only possibilities in such positions."

35...♗e8! 36 b4!

The idea behind Black's last move is that 36 ♘xd6 ♘xd6 37 ♖xd6 ♛xd6 38 ♛xa7 ♛b4! gives counterplay.

36...a4 37 ♔h2 ♖aa8 38 ♗e2 ♖c7 39 b5 ♛d8

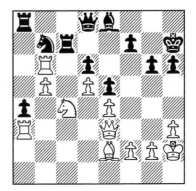

40 ♖a2

Black's last move prevented 40 f4 because of 40...exf4 41 ♕xf4 ♖xc4 42 ♖xb7 ♖c7 – he's certainly making it as difficult as possible for White to score the full point.

40...♔g7

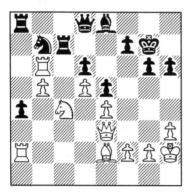

41 ♖c6

Bronstein's sealed move, the only problem with it being that it cost 35 minutes on the clock.

41...♖b8

Here too Bronstein sank into thought after, according to Keres, being visibly surprised by Black's last move. If 41...♗xc6 42 dxc6 ♘c5 White would have had 43 ♘xe5.

42 ♖d2!

Once again Bronstein avoids one of the pitfalls in the position. After 42 ♖xa4 Black would play 42...♗xc6 43 dxc6 ♘c5 44 ♖a5 ♘e6 when the knight can come to d4.

42...h5 43 ♖d1

There was a good chance for White to wrap things up here. 43 ♕c3! would have been decisive due to the many threats (♘xd6, ♘xe5, f4), though this takes nothing away from Black's re-

sourceful defence which made things as difficult as possible for White.

43...♔g8 44 ♔g1 ♔h7 45 ♕a3 ♕e7

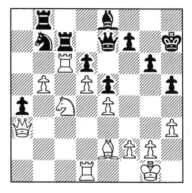

46 ♕xa4?

Bronstein used up additional time on the line 46 ♘xd6 ♗xc6 47 dxc6 ♘xd6 48 ♕xd6 (48 ♖xd6 ♖d8 49 ♖d3 ♕xa3 50 ♖xa3 ♖d4 followed by ...♖b4 isn't easy either) 48...♕xd6 49 ♖xd6 a3 50 ♖d2 ♖a7. However, 46 ♕c3! was strong.

46...♘c5

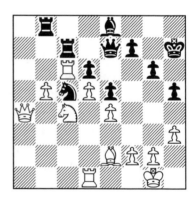

47 ♕c2?!

White should have played 47 ♕a5 when 47...♗xc6 (47...♖a7! is better) 48 dxc6 ♘xe4 49 ♗f3 would have been good for him.

47...♗xc6! 48 dxc6 ♖xb5!

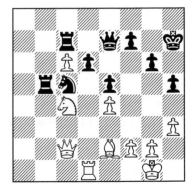

49 ♘xd6

White could still draw with 49 ♘e3! ♖b8 50 ♘d5 ♕d8 51 ♘xc7 ♕xc7 52 ♗c4. After the text move he has to be very careful.

49...♖b6

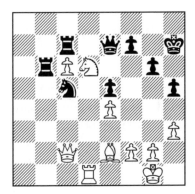

50 ♗b5?

With 50 ♕xc5 ♖cxc6 51 ♕xb6 ♖xb6 52 ♘c8 ♕c5 53 ♘xb6 ♕xb6 White should hold with careful defence.

50...♘e6 51 ♗a4 ♘d4 52 ♕c5 ♖bxc6! 53 ♗xc6 ♖xc6 0-1

White lost on time here, but the position is hopeless anyway.

40) Middlegame understanding helps your opening

A common problem for many players is that they 'learn' a few opening moves but are then clueless as to how to play the resulting middlegame. There is only one antidote that I know of and that is to focus on typical middlegame strategies and then show how the opening moves fit into such set-ups by bringing about particular middlegame positions. It follows that if a player has a good understanding of certain middlegame positions he will know where his pieces should be headed in the opening.

One of the classic plans in chess is the minority attack. This involves levering open a half-open file with a pawn, the best known example being in the Queen's Gambit Declined Exchange Variation. The following game snippet shows the idea.

Game 51
S.Reshevsky-L.Myagmarsuren
Sousse Interzonal 1967
Queen's Gambit Declined

---

1 d4 e6 2 c4 d5 3 ♘c3 ♘f6 4 cxd5 exd5 5 ♗g5 ♗e7 6 e3 0-0 7 ♗d3 c6 8 ♕c2 ♘bd7 9 ♘f3 ♖e8 10 0-0 ♘f8 11 ♗xf6 ♗xf6

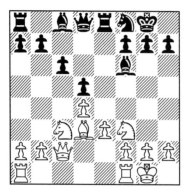

Here White played:

12 b4!

This sets up a minority attack.

12...♗g4 13 ♘d2 ♖c8 14 ♗f5 ♗xf5 15 ♕xf5 g6 16 ♕d3 ♕d6 17 ♖fb1! ♗g7 18 a4 ♘d7 19 ♖a2 ♖e6 20 ♖c2 ♖ce8 21 ♘b3 ♘f6?! 22 h3 b6? 23 ♘c1 ♗h6 24 ♘1e2 ♘h5

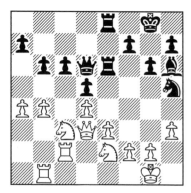

25 b5!

A key move in the minority attack. Whatever Black does he will be left with a pawn weakness, and White soon reached a winning position.

So let us imagine that in the next game Black knows very little about the Caro-Kann but he has at least seen some games with this plan. He will find it easy to play the opening because he knows what to play for, an undermining of White's queenside pawns with ...b7-b5-b4. This is how the middlegame can help your opening play and why the opening should be studied from the point of view of complete games.

1 e4 c6 2 d4 d5 3 exd5 cxd5 4 ♗d3 ♘c6 5 c3 ♘f6 6 ♗f4 ♗g4 7 ♕b3

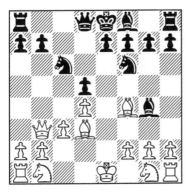

7...♕d7!?

An interesting alternative to both 7...♕c8 and 7...♘a5.

8 ♘d2 e6 9 ♘gf3 ♗xf3 10 ♘xf3 ♗d6 11 ♗xd6

11 ♘e5 looks tempting but the knight is unstable on this square. After

11...♕c7 12 0-0 0-0 13 ♖ae1 ♘h5 White is suddenly in trouble.

11...♕xd6 12 0-0

After 12 ♕xb7 ♖b8 13 ♕a6 0-0 Black gets adequate counterplay for the pawn. For example, 14 ♗b5 ♖b6 15 ♕a4 ♘e7 16 0-0 ♕b8 17 ♗d3 ♖xb2 and Black recovers his pawn with equal play; 14 ♖b1?! is strongly met by 14...♖b6 15 ♕a4 e5!; and 14 0-0 offers White nothing better than equality after 14...♖b6 15 ♕a3 ♕xa3 16 bxa3.

12...0-0 13 ♖ae1

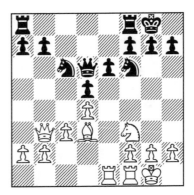

13...♖ab8 14 ♘e5 b5

Black gets his minority attack underway. More usually these positions occur with reversed colours, as in Game 51.

15 ♖e3

On 15 ♗xb5 Black can play 15...♘xd4! (15...♘e7 16 ♕a4) 16 cxd4 a6 and recover his piece with a good game.

15...b4 16 ♕c2 ♖fc8 17 ♕e2

White has a tempting sacrifice in 17 ♗xh7+? ♘xh7 18 ♘xf7 but Black can refute it with 18...♕f4.

17...bxc3 18 bxc3 ♕d8! 19 ♖h3 g6

Securing his kingside against the threat of 20 ♗xh7+.

20 f4 ♘e7 21 ♕e1?

This could be the decisive mistake. White should play the energetic 21 g4! after which 21...♖xc3 22 ♕e1 ♖c7 23 ♕h4 ♘c6 24 f5 gives White a dangerous attack for the sacrificed pawn.

Following the text move Black manages to shore up his defences after which White's queenside weaknesses are the only show in town.

21...h5! 22 ♔h1

Black's last move neutralized the possibility of 22 g4?!, which is met by 22...♘xg4 23 ♘xg4 hxg4 24 ♖h6 ♔g7 25 ♕h4 ♕g8 etc.

22...♖b2 23 a4 ♔g7

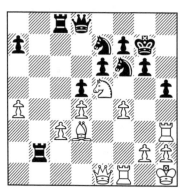

24 ♖g1?!

In time trouble White's resistance crumbles. Continuing the attack with g2-g4 is unrealistic here.

24...♘f5 25 ♕a1

After 25 g4 hxg4 26 ♘xg4 ♘xg4 27 ♖xg4 ♕f6 Black would defend everything, leaving White's position full of holes.

25...♕b6 26 a5 ♕b3 27 ♗xf5

The tricky 27 c4 (threatening 28 ♗xf5) would have been answered by 27...♘g4!.

27...exf5 28 ♘d3

This time 28 c4 is met by 28...♘e4 threatening smothered mate on f2.

28...♖a2

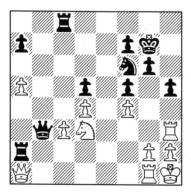

29 ♕f1

After 29 ♘c1 Black's 29...♘e4 (threatening mate on f2) is once again a crusher.

29...♘e4 30 ♘c1 ♕c2 31 ♖f3 ♖xa5 32 ♕e1 ♖a1 33 h3 ♖xc3

The pawns are falling like flies.

34 ♖xc3 ♕xc3 35 ♕xc3 ♘xc3 36 ♔h2 a5 37 ♖e1 a4 0-1

Chapter Five

The Endgame

In my work as a chess coach it has been very noticeable that the endgame tends to be the weakest area for most players at club level. There are probably several reasons for this: first of all endgames are more rarely reached at amateur level, and when they are there may not be much time left on the clock. There is also the factor that endgames are often perceived as being dull compared to the middlegame.

Whatever the reason, this makes the endgame the area of chess where players can most quickly develop superior skills to those of their opponents. This in turn can provide a rich dividend of points. As a strong club player once put it to me, if all else failed he would exchange queens after which his winning chances would improve dramatically.

There are also many hidden benefits to studying the endgame which many players are unaware of. First of all it can improve your middlegame play by making your decisions more measured and relaxed. No longer dependent on checkmate to win a game, players are less likely to overreach.

A second advantage is that players who study endgames learn to appreciate the powers of the individual pieces. Such *micro-patterns* can then be subconsciously applied to all sorts of different opening and middlegame scenarios. For example, a player may instinctively understand that a bishop and knight coordinate better on particular squares because this intuition was built up by a study of the endgame. Such factors tend to be overlooked by players who try to ape the most fashionable opening variations.

In this section I have presented a selection of rules that address many of the misunderstandings I have witnessed over the years.

41) Use the king

"The King is a strong piece."

Wilhelm Steinitz

Steinitz was right; the king is a strong piece, though I would not advise going as far as Steinitz used to do to 'prove' this. For example Steinitz's line of the King's Gambit went 1 e4 e5 2 f4 exf4 3 ♘c3 with the idea of luring Black into playing 3...♕h4+ and answering with 4 ♔e2. On a board full of pieces even the strongest king can find himself overwhelmed by a number of weaker pieces.

As pieces are exchanged and the endgame approaches, the danger of mate gradually diminishes. This in turn allows the king to use his strength (roughly equivalent to that of a rook) in an active and aggressive way.

In the following example White's king plays a decisive role by invading Black's position on the kingside and forcing the win of some pawns.

Game 53
M.Dvoretsky-V.Smyslov
USSR Championship,
Odessa 1974
Ruy Lopez

1 e4 e5 2 ♘f3 ♘c6 3 ♗b5 a6 4 ♗xc6 dxc6 5 0-0 ♕e7 6 d4 exd4 7 ♕xd4 ♗g4 8 ♗f4 ♗xf3 9 gxf3 ♘f6 10 ♘c3 ♘h5 11 ♗g3 ♖d8 12 ♕e3 ♘xg3 13 hxg3 ♕c5 14 ♖ad1 ♕xe3 15 ♖xd8+ ♔xd8 16 ♖d1+ ♔c8 17 fxe3

This is a typical Exchange Spanish endgame in which White is better because his pawn majority can more easily yield a passed pawn. Of course with a great endgame specialist like Vasily Smyslov playing Black, one would expect some very stubborn resistance, but

just watch what happens here:

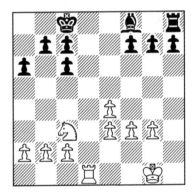

17...g6?

This allows White to set up a powerful bind on the kingside. Just 17...♗e7 would have been stronger, or maybe 17...♗b4 18 ♘e2 ♖e8.

18 e5 ♗g7 19 f4 f6

Otherwise White plays 20 ♘e4.

20 exf6 ♗xf6 21 e4 h5 22 ♔g2

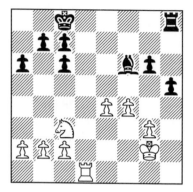

22...♗xc3

22...h4 was worth considering, both here and on the next move. In this instance White would have the advantage after 23 e5 ♗e7 24 ♘e4 hxg3 25 ♔xg3, but this is by no means as bad as the game turns out.

23 bxc3 b5

Here too 23...h4!? might have been a better shot, the point being that 24 ♖h1

can be answered by 24...♖d8.

24 e5 a5 25 ♔h3!

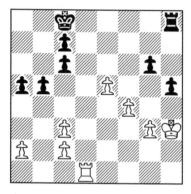

The start of an awesome display of king power. His majesty is en route for g5 and then h6, causing devastation to Black's kingside pawns.

25...b4 26 ♔h4 ♖e8 27 ♔g5 ♖e6 28 ♔h6 1-0

There is no defence to 29 ♔g7 and 30 ♔f7.

42) Rooks belong on the seventh

The rook comes into its own in the endgame. Without the presence of so many pawns or the problem of being harassed by pieces of lesser value, rooks can take a much more active role in the game.

Of particular note is the placement of a rook on the seventh rank from where it can fulfil several different functions. First of all it can tie down the opposing king if that is still on the back rank. Secondly it can attack any enemy pawns which have yet to move. And thirdly it can get *behind* the opponent's passed pawns.

This final consideration is particularly important because the rook will become more active as the passed pawn advances. If, on the other hand, it goes in front of the passed pawn its mobility will be restricted ever more as the pawn advances.

I was deeply impressed by the following game in which Petrosian gave up a pawn to get his rook to the seventh rank.

Game 54
T.Petrosian-L.Portisch
Candidates Quarter-final
(13th game),
Palma de Mallorca 1974
Queen's Gambit Declined

---

1 ♘f3 d5 2 d4 e6 3 c4 ♘f6 4 ♗g5 ♗e7 5 ♘c3 0-0 6 ♖c1 h6 7 ♗h4 b6 8 cxd5 ♘xd5 9 ♘xd5 exd5 10 ♗xe7 ♕xe7 11 g3 ♗a6 12 e3 c5 13 ♗xa6 ♘xa6 14 0-0 ♘c7 15 b3 ♖ac8 16 ♖e1 ♖fd8 17 h4 ♘e6 18 ♕d3 ♕f6 19 ♔g2 cxd4 20 exd4 ♖xc1 21 ♖xc1

White may have the tiniest of advantages here because his rook controls the open c-file. Of course his inability to get the rook to the seventh rank, because of the knight on e6, limits the size of this advantage. With his next move Portisch decides to try and force

complete 'equality', but in doing so he misses a concealed possibility.

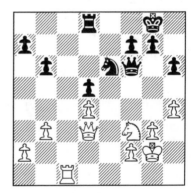

21...♕f4?!

At first sight this looks excellent, attacking the rook on c1 whilst preparing to bring the queen either to e4 or maybe back to d6. White of course cannot take the queen because he would lose a pawn when the knight recaptures and forks. Or can he?

22 gxf4!

Sacrificing a pawn in order to penetrate Black's position with his rook.

22...♘xf4+ 23 ♔g3 ♘xd3 24 ♖c3

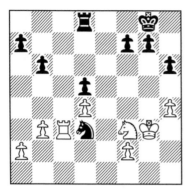

24...♘b4

In his notes to the game, endgame specialist Yuri Averbakh suggested that Black can draw with 24...♘b2, but this seems better for White after 25 h5! intending 26 ♖c7 and 27 ♘e5.

25 a3 ♘a6 26 b4 ♘b8?

After this move Black is in serious trouble. Averbakh suggested two other possibilities:

a) 26...♖d7!? 27 ♖c8+ ♔h7 28 b5 (28 h5!? seems interesting, making Black's king bad) 28...♘c7 29 ♘e5 ♖e7 30 ♘c6 ♖d7 31 ♘xa7 ♘e8.

b) 26...♔h7!? 27 b5 (I like 27 h5!? here too) 27...♘b8 28 ♖c7 ♖d7 29 ♖c8 ♖b7.

These are certainly improvements but Black, but White is still pressing in all lines.

27 ♖c7 a5 28 b5 ♘d7 29 ♔f4

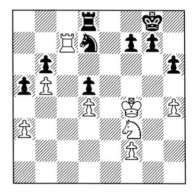

29...h5

As a last ditch attempt to save the game for Black.

Averbakh gave 29...♘f8, after which 30 ♖b7 ♘e6+ 31 ♔e5 ♘f8 32 ♔f4 ♘e6+ would repeat the position. But here too White can try to squeeze more out of it with 32 h5.

30 ♘e5 ♘f8 31 ♖b7 f6 32 ♘c6 ♘g6+

The line 32...♖e8 33 ♖xb6 ♖e4+ 34 ♔g3 ♖g4+ 35 ♔f3 ♘e6 would give Black counterplay, but White can first play 33 ♔g3.

33 ♔g3 ♖d6 34 ♖xb6 ♖e6 35 ♖b8+ ♘f8 36 ♖a8 ♖e1 37 ♘d8 ♔h7 38 b6 ♖b1 39 b7 ♘d7 40 ♖xa5 1-0

43) Passed pawns should be pushed

"The passed Pawn is a criminal, who should be kept under lock and key. Mild measures, such as police surveillance, are not sufficient."

Aron Nimzowitsch (*My System*)

Besides kings and rooks, the third piece that comes into its own in the endgame is the humble pawn. With fewer pieces remaining on the board they will more easily be able to advance. Their value as a proportion of the material left on the board will also increase considerably, especially as their odds of being promoted increase.

Here is one of the most famous and picturesque examples of passed pawns deciding a game.

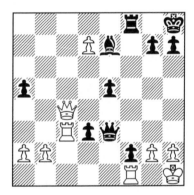

Game 55
A.McDonnell-L.De Labourdonnais
London (16th matchgame) 1834
Sicilian Defence

1 e4 c5 2 ♘f3 ♘c6 3 d4 cxd4 4 ♘xd4 e5 5 ♘xc6 bxc6 6 ♗c4 ♘f6 7 ♗g5 ♗e7 8 ♕e2 d5 9 ♗xf6 ♗xf6 10 ♗b3 0-0 11 0-0 a5 12 exd5 cxd5 13 ♖d1 d4 14 c4 ♕b6 15 ♗c2 ♗b7 16 ♘d2 ♖ae8 17 ♘e4 ♗d8 18 c5 ♕c6 19 f3 ♗e7 20 ♖ac1 f5 21 ♕c4+ ♔h8 22 ♗a4 ♕h6 23 ♗xe8 fxe4 24 c6 exf3 25 ♖c2 ♕e3+ 26 ♔h1 ♗c8 27 ♗d7 f2 28 ♖f1 d3 29 ♖c3 ♗xd7 30 cxd7

Both sides have passed pawns in this position but Black has rather more of them. The finish is a most pleasing demonstration of the power of these little monsters once they start to roll down the board.

30...e4! 31 ♕c8 ♗d8

31...♖d8 might have made things a bit easier but there is nothing wrong with the move played.

32 ♕c4 ♕e1 33 ♖c1 d2 34 ♕c5

Threatening to take the rook and mate on f8.

34...♖g8 35 ♖d1 e3! 36 ♕c3 ♕xd1!

The most elegant way to finish matters.

37 ♖xd1 e2 0-1

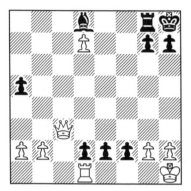

A beautiful and famous final position. At least a couple of Black's pawns will promote, delivering checkmate in the process.

The corollary of this rule is that when facing a passed pawn or pawns they should be blockaded, and indeed great strength can then be derived from this blockade as the enemy pawns can be the most effective shield for the blockading pieces. The following game is a wonderful example of this, with Pilnik giving his famous adversary two connected passed pawns in an endgame. But because they were firmly blockaded, the pawns were the source of White's problems.

> ### Game 56
> ### M.Euwe-H.Pilnik
> Amsterdam 1950
> *Grünfeld Defence*

1 d4 ♞f6 2 c4 g6 3 g3 ♝g7 4 ♝g2 d5 5 cxd5 ♞xd5 6 e4 ♞b6 7 ♞e2 c5 8 d5 0-0 9 0-0 e6 10 ♞bc3?!

10 a4 and 10 ♞ec3 are now thought to be better moves.
10...♞a6 11 ♞f4 e5 12 ♞fe2

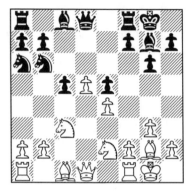

12...♞c4!
With the emergence of a passed white d-pawn, Black's knight heads for the blockade square on d6. White should now have tried to cut across this plan with 13 ♞b5 ♝d7 14 ♞ec3 ♛b6 15 a4 or 13...♞c7 14 ♛c2!.
13 b3?! ♞d6 14 ♝e3 b6 15 ♛d2 ♜e8

A prophylactic idea against White's next move, which he would therefore have been better to avoid.

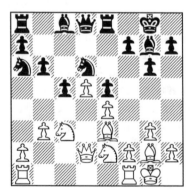

16 f4?!
White should have contented him-

self with 16 f3, just lending more support to the e4-pawn.

16...♘c7

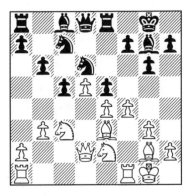

17 ♖f2?

A serious mistake because now White has to concede the e5-square. 17 ♖ae1 would have been better, after which White can meet 17...exf4 with 18 gxf4.

17...exf4! 18 ♗xf4

Now White is unable to recapture with the g-pawn because 18 gxf4? is answered by 18...♘xe4 19 ♗xe4 ♖xe4 etc.

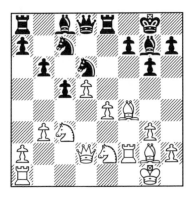

18...♗a6

In this position 18...♘xe4? would be

inadvisable because of 19 ♗xe4 ♖xe4 20 ♘xe4 ♗xa1 21 ♘2c3! with a powerful attack on the dark squares coming.

19 ♖e1 ♕e7 20 g4 ♗e5!

The blockading pieces on d6 and e5 are immensely strong.

21 ♗xe5 ♕xe5 22 ♘g3?

White should try to challenge for control of the e5-square with 22 ♔h1 intending ♘e2-g1-f3.

22...♖e7 23 ♗f1 ♗c8 24 ♗e2 ♗d7 25 ♖ef1 ♖f8 26 ♕c1 ♘ce8 27 ♔h1 f6 28 ♖g1 ♘g7?!

Black should have played 28...♘f7 intending 29...♘ed6. But even after the move played he is better.

29 ♗f3?!

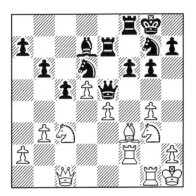

29 h4 would have stopped Black's next move which turns out to be a real corker.

29...♕g5!

A really superb positional move. Black gives his opponent two connected passed pawns, but they will both be blockaded.

30 ♕xg5 fxg5 31 ♖gf1 ♘ge8 32 ♗e2 ♖xf2 33 ♖xf2 ♔g7 34 h3 ♘f6 35 ♗f3 ♗e8 36 ♖e2 ♘d7 37 ♖d2 ♘e5!

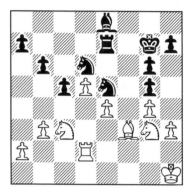

Now everything starts to become clear. White's passed pawns are blockaded and Black can easily advance his own majority on the queenside. The rest of the game is nicely conducted by Pilnik.

38 ♗e2 b5! 39 ♖c2 ♖c7 40 ♘d1 c4 41 bxc4 bxc4 42 ♘c3 ♔f6 43 ♘b1 ♖b7 44 ♘d2 ♗a4! 45 ♖c1 ♖b2 46 ♘xc4 ♘exc4 47 ♗xc4 ♗c2! 48 ♗b3 ♖b1 49 ♖xb1 ♗xb1 50 ♘e2 ♗xe4+ 51 ♔h2 ♔e5 52 ♘c3 ♗d3 53 ♔g3 ♘e4+ 54 ♘xe4 ♗xe4 55 d6 ♔xd6 56 ♗g8 h6 57 ♗f7 ♗d5 58 ♗xg6 ♗xa2 59 h4 a5 60 hxg5 hxg5 61 ♔f3 a4 62 ♔e3 ♗e6 63 ♔d4 ♗xg4 64 ♔c3 ♗d1 65 ♗f5 ♔e5 66 ♗d7 ♔f4 67 ♔b4 ♗c2 68 ♔c3 ♗b3 69 ♔b4 ♗f7 70 ♔xa4 ♗g6 71 ♔b4 ♗f5! 72 ♗c6 g4 73 ♔c5 ♗e4 74 ♗d7 g3 75 ♗h3 ♔e3 76 ♔d6 ♗f5! 77 ♗g2 ♔f2 0-1

44) Do not hurry

"The ability to make use of this principle demands of a player great experience in the playing of chess endings. How many endings have not been won, merely because the stronger side tried to win as quickly as possible, and neglected to make simple strengthening moves before embarking on positive action."

Mikhail Shereshevsky (*Endgame Strategy*)

This principle is an important one for cultivating the right mentality for playing the endgame. Gradually improving a position not only helps to squeeze the most out of it; it is also psychological torture for the opponent. An unhurried approach will often provoke further mistakes by a tired and frustrated opponent, making the win much quicker than a rushed attempt at victory.

Here is a masterful example of this rule in action, Salo Flohr grinding his opponent down very effectively:

Game 57
S.Flohr-I.Bondarevsky
Leningrad/Moscow 1939
Dutch Defence

---

1 d4 e6 2 c4 f5 3 g3 ♘f6 4 ♗g2 ♗b4+ 5 ♗d2 ♗e7 6 ♕b3 d5 7 ♘f3 c6 8 0-0 0-0 9 ♗b4 ♘e4 10 ♘bd2 ♘d7 11 ♗xe7 ♕xe7 12 ♖ac1 ♔h8 13 ♕e3 ♘df6 14 ♘e5 ♘xd2 15 ♕xd2 ♗d7 16 a3 ♗e8 17 ♕e3 ♔g8 18 ♘d3 dxc4 19 ♖xc4 ♖d8 20 ♘e5 ♘d5 21 ♗xd5 exd5 22 ♖c3 f4 23 gxf4 ♕h4 24 ♕g3 ♕xf4 25 ♕xf4 ♖xf4 26 e3 ♖f6 27 ♖b3 ♖b8 28 f3 ♔f8 29 ♔f2 ♖h6 30 ♔g3 ♔e7 31 ♖c3 ♖d8 32 h4 ♗d7 33 ♖c2 g5 34 hxg5 ♖h3+ 35 ♔g2 ♖h5 36 ♖h1 ♖xg5+ 37 ♔f1 ♗f5 38 ♖g2 ♖dg8 39 ♖xg5 ♖xg5 40 ♔f2 ♔f6 41 ♖h4 ♖g7 42 b4 ♔g5 43 ♖h1 ♔f6 44 ♖h2 ♖g5

White is better here because of his strongly placed knight on e5 and the fact that Black's queenside pawn majority is difficult to mobilize. Can this possibly be enough to win? Perhaps not against best defence, but Flohr gives a magnificent demonstration of how to make the most of White's advantages. And his watchword is not to hurry.

45 a4 ♖g7 46 a5

Threatening to undermine Black's c6-pawn with 47 a6. Black can stop this by playing ...a7-a6 himself, but this would lead to his queenside pawns being crippled and give White's knight an even better outpost on c5.

46...罝c7

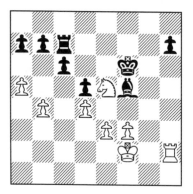

47 罝h6+!

A very instructive move. White wants to bring his rook to c1 but rather than play the immediate 47 罝h1 he first takes the opportunity to worsen Black's position. Such patient play is the hallmark of a great endgame master.

47...鼻g6 48 罝h1

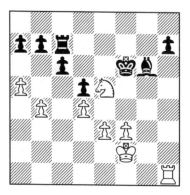

48...鼻f5?

This may already be the decisive mistake. Black should try 48...b6 in this position as he now gets his queenside pawns fixed on light squares.

49 罝c1 a6

Forced because of the threat of 50 a6, and from White's point of view this is a major accomplishment. With Black's queenside pawns fixed and immobile, White can turn his attention to creating his own passed e-pawn.

50 罝h1 鼻g7 51 罝h2!

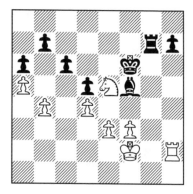

Once again Flohr is in no hurry. Black's pieces are currently on their best squares so White invites him to worsen them by making another move.

51...罝c7 52 罝h6+ 鼻g6 53 罝h4 鼻f5

Or 53...鼻g5 54 罝g4+ followed by 55 e4.

54 e4 dxe4 55 fxe4 鼻g6 56 罝f4+ 鼻e6 57 鼻e3!

Once again a nice patient move, improving the white king. White's plan here is to bring his knight to the c5-square from where it bears down on b7 and supports an advance of White's e-pawn. But why hurry?

57...♖g7 58 ♘d3 ♔d6 59 ♘c5 ♖e7 60 ♖f8

This move threatens 61 ♖b8 winning the b7-pawn.

60...♔c7 61 e5

61...♖e8

After having been tortured for quite a while Black tries to relieve his agony by exchanging rooks. Unfortunately for him the minor piece endgame is lost, which becomes clear when the h-pawn falls.

62 ♖xe8 ♗xe8 63 ♔f4 b6 64 ♘a4 bxa5 65 bxa5 ♗f7 66 ♘c5 ♗c4 67 ♔g5 ♗e2 68 ♔h6 ♔d8 69 ♔xh7 ♔e7 70 ♔g6 ♗f1 71 ♔f5

Even at this stage White is in no hurry. He sees that the most secure way to win the game is to bring his king to c5.

71...♗h3+ 72 ♔e4 ♗g2+ 73 ♔e3 ♗f1 74 ♔d2 ♔f7 75 ♔c3 ♔g6 76 ♔b4 ♔f5 77 ♘b7 1-0

An object lesson in patience.

45) Beware the point of no return!

One of the major features of endgames is that they can often be worked out to an arithmetically clear win, draw or loss. This means that they must usually be played with much greater precision than the opening or middlegame, and this in turn adds to their difficulty despite the reduction in material.

For this reason endgames should be played with great patience and care, mindful that the point of no return could occur at any time. A win can easily turn into a draw and a draw into a loss, as the following game tragically demonstrates.

Game 58
J.Carleton-S.Sulskis
European Union Championship,
Liverpool 2006

60 ♘f1?

It's not clear what White misses here but undoubtedly he should just hold on to the c4-pawn. 60 ♗b6 would leave Black with nothing, as after 60...♘f3 there is just 61 ♘f1.

60...♗xc4

60...♘xc4? 61 ♘d2+ would lead to a

drawn opposite-coloured bishop endgame.

61 ♘d2+ ♔d5 62 ♗b8 b5

63 ♗xe5?

In playing this and his next move it seems that White miscalculated the pawn endgame. 63 ♗c7 is a better chance, keeping both sets of minor pieces on the board.

63...♔xe5 64 ♘xc4+?

Losing very simply. 64 ♘b1 would at least put up a fight: for example, 64...♔e4 65 ♘a3 ♔f3 66 ♘c2 ♔g2 67 ♘e3+ ♔h3 68 ♔b4 ♔h4 69 ♔c5 makes it difficult for Black to win.

64...bxc4 65 ♔xc4

(see following diagram)

65...♔e4! 0-1

This looks like what White missed in playing 64 ♘xc4+, probably expecting 65...♔f4? 66 ♔d4 ♔f3 67 ♔e5 ♔g2 68 ♔f4 with a draw.

After 65...♔e4! he is completely lost, for example 66 ♔c5 ♔f3 67 ♔d5 ♔g2 68 ♔e5 ♔xh2 etc.

46) Queen and knight, they're alright

Queen and knight have been known to cooperate well together for some time, but it was British chess players who came up with the catchy jingo that encapsulates this idea.

Queen and knight cooperate particularly well together because they complement rather than duplicate each other's activity. So if you have a knight against a bishop in the middlegame it makes sense to favour the exchange of pieces other than the queens. And if you have the bishop then probably you should be happy to allow the exchange of queens but keep other pieces on.

Here's an illustration of the strength of queen and knight against queen and bishop.

> **Game 59**
> **Vl.Jansa-A.Hennings**
> Karlovy Vary 1973
> *Ruy Lopez*

first of all the natural tendency of a queen and knight to cooperate well together; and secondly Black's weaknesses on the dark squares. Even so it is surprising how quickly he manages to win.

1 e4 e5 2 ♘f3 ♘c6 3 ♗b5 a6 4 ♗a4 ♘f6 5 0-0 ♗e7 6 ♖e1 b5 7 ♗b3 d6 8 c3 0-0 9 h3 ♘b8 10 d3 ♘bd7 11 ♘bd2 ♗b7 12 ♘f1 ♘c5 13 ♗c2 ♖e8 14 ♘g3 ♗f8 15 b4 ♘cd7 16 d4 ♘b6 17 ♗d3 g6 18 ♗d2 ♗g7 19 ♕c2 ♖c8 20 ♖ad1 c6 21 dxe5 dxe5 22 c4 bxc4 23 ♗xc4 ♘xc4 24 ♕xc4 ♕c7 25 ♖c1 ♘d7 26 ♗e3 ♘f8 27 ♘d2 ♘e6 28 ♘b3 ♗f8 29 ♘e2 ♖ed8 30 ♘c3 ♕d6 31 ♘c5 ♘xc5 32 ♗xc5 ♕c7 33 ♘a4 ♗xc5 34 ♘xc5 ♖d4 35 ♕c3 ♖cd8 36 ♘b3 ♖d3 37 ♕c5 h5 38 ♖e3 ♖d1+ 39 ♔h2 ♖xc1 40 ♕xc1 ♕e7 41 ♘c5 ♖d4 42 ♖d3 ♗c8 43 ♖xd4 exd4

Material is level, with a queen and a minor piece for both sides. But White has two advantages in this position:

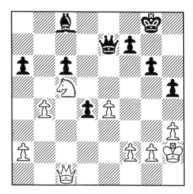

44 ♕f4 ♗e6! 45 a3!?

And not 45 ♕e5? because of 45...♕d8! when 46 ♘xe6 fxe6 47 ♕xe6+ ♔g7 allows Black to draw the queen endgame because of his powerful passed d-pawn.

45...♗c4?

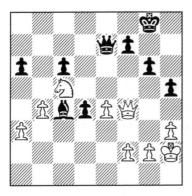

The decisive mistake, allowing White to seize key dark squares on the kingside.

Black should have tried 45...♕d8 when 46 e5 d3 47 ♘e4 ♔g7 is still better for White but by no means clearly winning.

46 e5! ♕d8 47 ♘e4

Threatening 48 ♕h6.

47...♔h7 48 ♘d6 ♗d5 49 ♘xf7 ♕f8 50 ♘g5+ ♔g7 51 ♕xd4

With two pawns falling in quick succession it's all over bar the shouting.

51...♕f5 52 h4 ♔g8 53 e6 ♕f8 54 ♔g1 a5 55 ♕a7 ♕f4 56 ♕h7+ ♔f8 57 ♕h8+ ♔e7 58 ♕g7+ 1-0

47) Opposite-coloured bishops don't always draw

A popular misconception amongst many players is that opposite-coloured bishops necessarily lead to a draw. It is certainly true that they sometimes do a superb job of blockading opposing pawns, often negating a two- or even three-pawn advantage. Yet this is not always the case and they can even help to generate winning chances for the player who has the initiative.

Why is this so? Because opposite-coloured bishops can help to attack squares that the opponent cannot defend. So add a rook to each side and these positions are not drawish at all.

The following endgame really impressed me, having been played in a tournament in which I took part. I could hardly believe that Black managed to win against such a capable opponent as Stefan Kindermann. And Gurevich even made it look rather easy.

> **Game 60**
> **S.Kindermann-M.Gurevich**
> Budapest 1987
> *French Defence*

1 e4 e6 2 d4 d5 3 ᵕc3 ᵕf6 4 ♗g5 ♗b4 5 exd5 ♕xd5 6 ♗xf6 gxf6 7 ♕d2 ♕a5 8 ♗d3 c5 9 ᵕf3 ᵕc6 10 dxc5 ♗d7 11 0-0 ♕xc5 12 ᵕe4 ♗xd2 13 ᵕxc5 ♗b4 14 ᵕxd7 ♔xd7 15 ♖fd1 ♔e7 16 ♗e4 ♖ac8 17 ᵕd4 ♗d6 18 ᵕxc6+ bxc6 19 ♖d3 ♗e5 20 ♖ad1 ♖c7 21 b4 f5 22 ♗f3 ♖b8 23 a3 a5 24 ♖b3 axb4 25 axb4 ♖b6 26 c4

With opposite-coloured bishops and level pawns it's difficult to believe this position can be anything other than a draw. In fact at first sight one might even prefer White's chances because of what seems like a more mobile

pawn majority on the queenside. But the truth is that Black actually has some chances here *because of* the opposite-colour bishops and the possibility of anchoring Black's on the powerful d4-square.

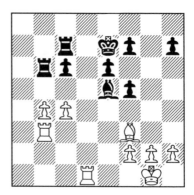

26...c5!

At first sight this looks like a terrible move, as it gives White a protected passed pawn with the rook on b6 being

---

reduced to the role of blockader. But the capture of the d4-square is far more important, and from there Black's bishop will bear down on f2.

27 b5 ♖a7 28 ♗c6?

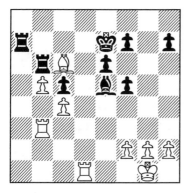

Preventing the rook on b6 from coming to d6, and supporting a white rook invasion on d7. But if White had fully understood the dangers of his position he might have played 28 g3 to start improving his king position. After 28...♖a4 29 ♖c1 ♖a2 30 ♖e3 ♗d4 31 ♖e2 White can defend himself.

28...♖a4 29 ♖h3

The passive 29 ♖c1 would be answered by 29...♖a2 30 ♔f1 ♗d4, when Black has all the chances.

29...♖xc4 30 ♖xh7 ♗d4 31 ♖h3 ♖c2 32 ♖f3

With White tied down to the f2-pawn he is now clearly worse. Black improves his position by activating the other rook.

32...♖b8 33 h4 ♖b2 34 ♖c1 ♖g8 35 ♔f1 ♖g4 36 g3 f4

Breaking up White's kingside pawns.

37 gxf4 ♖xh4 38 ♔g2 f5 39 ♖c4 ♖b1 40 ♖a4?!

40 ♖c2 would have resisted more stubbornly, but Black is still better after 40...♔d6.

40...♖g4+ 41 ♖g3 ♖xf4 42 ♖a2 c4 43 ♖e2 c3 0-1

48) Two bishops are better than none

"The contribution of the two bishops is extremely powerful and controls the whole board. They cannot be compared with the two rooks, for their efforts cannot concentrate on one object; but they are very strong in the end game, when they work in two directions, threatening both wings. The two bishops can literally tie up the opposing forces. In examples of the contest between two bishops and other minor pieces it may seem surprising that the adversary's position in most cases tends to be restricted: but it is the result of the preliminary action of the bishops, which is slow and methodical."

Eugene Znosko-Borovsky (*How to Play Chess Endings*)

The complementary effects of queen and knight working together are echoed with the two bishops. It's very rare that any other combination of minor pieces will prove stronger than this one, especially in the endgame. And against two knights they tend to be especially strong.

In the following game it seems that White has one of the least advantageous two-bishop situations because the position is blocked. Even so, they prove to be a potent force.

Game 61
S.Flohr-M.Botvinnik
Moscow/Leningrad
(6th matchgame) 1933
Nimzo-Indian Defence

---

1 d4 ♘f6 2 c4 e6 3 ♘c3 ♗b4 4 ♕c2 c5 5 dxc5 ♘a6 6 a3 ♗xc3+ 7 ♕xc3 ♘xc5 8 f3 d6 9 e4 e5 10 ♗e3 ♕c7 11 ♘e2 ♗e6 12 ♕c2 0-0 13 ♘c3 ♖fc8 14 ♗e2 a6 15 ♖c1 ♘cd7 16 ♕d2 ♕b8 17 ♘d5 ♗xd5 18 cxd5 ♖xc1+ 19 ♕xc1 ♕d8 20 0-0 ♖c8 21 ♕d2 ♕c7 22 ♖c1 ♕xc1+ 23 ♕xc1 ♖xc1+ 24 ♗xc1 ♔f8

White has two bishops against two knights but the blocked nature of the

position is going to make it difficult to activate them. Essentially White needs to open the game up before they can come into their own.

25 ♔f2 ♔e7 26 ♗e3 ♔d8 27 ♔e1 ♔c7 28 ♔d2 ♘c5 29 b4 ♘cd7?!

White's previous move drove the knight away from c5 but in doing so weakened the a4-square. Black could and should have tried to exploit this with 29...♘a4 followed by ...b7-b5.

White in turn should now play 30 a4 to prevent Black from carrying out this ...♘a4 and ...b5 plan.

30 g3?! ♘b6 31 ♔c2

31...♘bd7?!

Once again missing the chance to play 31...♘a4. Now White stops it once and for all.

32 a4! ♘b6 33 a5 ♘bd7 34 ♗c1 ♔d8 35 ♗b2 ♘e8 36 ♔d2

White has secured a space advantage on the queenside and marked out the b7-pawn as a weakness. Now he brings his king over to the other side of the board to support some action there.

36...♘c7 37 ♔e3 ♔e7 38 ♗f1 ♘b5 39 h4! ♘c7 40 ♗h3 ♘e8 41 f4

Putting pressure on the e5-pawn which provokes Black into creating further weaknesses.

41...f6 42 ♗f5! g6 43 ♗h3 h6

Preparing to meet 44 f5 with 44...g5. Botvinnik did not like 43...♘g7 be-

cause of 44 f5 (threatening 45 fxg6 followed by a later g3-g4 and h4-h5, getting a passed h-pawn) 44...g5 45 hxg5 fxg5 46 f6+ ♘xf6 47 ♗c8. But it seems that this is not that clear cut after 47...♘gh5: for example, 48 g4 ♔d8! 49 ♗xb7 ♘xg4+ gets two connected passed pawns on the g- and h-files.

44 ♗c1 ♘g7 45 fxe5 dxe5

And not 45...♘xe5 because of 46 ♗c8, or 45...fxe5 46 ♔f3 h5 47 ♗g5+ etc.

46 ♔f3 h5 47 ♗e3 ♔d6 48 ♗h6 ♘e8 49 g4

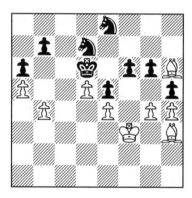

This is all very instructive: little by little White is breaking down the pawn structure that inhibits his bishop pair.

49...hxg4+ 50 ♗xg4 ♘c7 51 ♗e3 ♘b5 52 ♔e2 ♘c7

After 52...f5 53 exf5 ♘f6 White can play 54 fxg6!: for example, 54...♘xg4 55 g7 ♘f6 56 h5 ♘c3+ 57 ♔d3 ♘cxd5 58 h6 ♘e7 59 ♗c5+ etc.

53 ♔d3!

Zugzwang: 53...♘b5 is answered by 54 ♗e6 (threatening 55 ♗f7) 54...♔e7 55 ♗c5+ ♘xc5+ 56 bxc5 intending 56...♘d4 57 ♗c8 ♘b3 58 ♔c4 ♔d8 (58...♘xa5+ 59 ♔b4 wins immediately) 59 ♔xb3 ♔xc8

60 ♔c2 and White will win by bringing his king over to g4 and playing h4-h5.

53...f5 54 exf5 gxf5 55 ♗xf5 ♘xd5 56 ♗d2 ♘7f6 57 ♔c4 ♔c6 58 ♗g6 b5+ 59 ♔d3 ♘e7 60 ♗e4+ ♘ed5

60...♘xe4 is no improvement: 61 ♔xe4 ♔d6 62 h5 ♔e6 63 h6 ♔f7 64 h7 ♔g7 65 ♔xe5 and White will win Black's a6-pawn with his king.

61 ♗g5 ♘h5 62 ♗f3 ♘g3 63 ♗d2!

And not 63 h5? because of 63...♘xh5 64 ♗xh5 ♘xb4+ when Black has drawing chances.

63...♔d6 64 ♗g4

Threatening to come to the c8-square once again.

64...♘f6 65 ♗c8 ♔c6 66 ♗e1! e4+ 67 ♔d4 ♘gh5 68 ♗f5 ♔d6 69 ♗d2 1-0

The pawn on e4 is doomed and White has a powerful passed h-pawn plus two mighty bishops.

Of course as with any strategic feature one should not fall in love with the bishop pair. In the following game the Dutch Grandmaster Jan Hein Donner believed that the bishops would get him a draw in spite of being a pawn down, but he was in for a rude awakening.

Game 62
B.Larsen-J.Donner
BBC Master Game,
England 1977
Pirc Defence

1 e4 d6 2 d4 ♘f6 3 ♘c3 g6 4 ♘f3 ♗g7 5 ♗e2 0-0 6 0-0 ♗g4 7 ♗e3 ♘c6 8 ♕d2 e5 9 d5 ♘e7 10 ♖ad1 ♗d7 11 ♘e1 ♘c8 12 ♔h1 ♘b6 13 ♗g5 ♘a4?!

Giving up a pawn for inadequate compensation.

14 ♘xa4 ♗xa4 15 ♕b4 ♗d7 16 ♕xb7

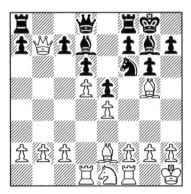

16...♕b8?

And this move simply astonished Larsen until he recalled Donner's belief that with the bishop pair you should be able to draw, even if a pawn down. Larsen goes on to show that this is decidedly not the case.

16...♖b8 was a better try: for example, 17 ♕xa7 ♖xb2 18 f3 ♕b8 19 ♕xb8 ♖fxb8 20 ♗c4 ♗b5 21 ♗xb5 ♖8xb5 22 a4 ♖a5 23 ♖a1 ♖b4 24 ♘d3 ♖bxa4 recovers the pawn and leaves Black just a bit worse.

17 ♕xb8 ♖axb8?! 18 ♗xf6 ♗xf6 19 b3 ♗e7 20 ♘d3 f5 21 ♗f3 a5 22 ♖fe1 a4 23 ♔g1 ♗g5 24 ♖e2 ♖b6 25 b4 a3

There's not much point getting opposite-coloured bishops via 25...♗b5, as rooks are still on the board.

26 c4 ♖a6 27 ♖b1 ♖a4 28 ♖b3 ♖b8 29 ♖c2 h5 30 g3 h4 31 ♗g2 ♖f8 32 gxh4 ♗xh4 33 ♖cc3! fxe4

If Black allowed himself be tied down with 33...♖fa8, White would pro-
-

ceed with 34 c5.

34 ♗xe4 ♗f5 35 f3

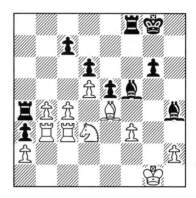

35...♗xe4 36 fxe4

The end of Black's bishop pair, and indeed Black might even have been relieved to have exchanged the monster on e4.

36...♖f3 37 c5 dxc5 38 ♖xc5 ♖e3 39 ♖a5! ♖xa5 40 bxa5 1-0

After 40...♖xe4 41 a6 ♖a4 42 ♖b4 ♖xb4 43 ♘xb4 ♗e7 44 ♘d3!, Black is unable to stop White's a-pawn.

49) Two weaknesses are better than one

"Appear where they cannot go, head for where they least expect you. To travel hundreds of miles without fatigue, go over land where there are no people."

Sun Tzu (*The Art of War*)

The idea of attacking two weaknesses is hardly unique to chess; it is universally applicable in all forms or warfare. When it is difficult to break through an opponent's defence by direct means, the correct strategy is to draw the defenders to a particular area of the board and then attack the sector that is left weak.

This strategy becomes particular important when there are relatively few pieces left on the board and the following game by Alexander Alekhine is a nice illustration. For a further example take a look at Donaldson-Taimanov (Game 13) from the 'Know yourself' section.

> ### Game 63
> **A.Alekhine-M.Vidmar**
> Hastings 1936/37
> Queen's Gambit Declined

1 d4 ♘f6 2 c4 e6 3 ♘c3 d5 4 ♗g5 ♘bd7 5 e3 ♗e7 6 ♘f3 0-0 7 ♖c1 c6 8 ♕c2 a6 9 cxd5 ♘xd5 10 ♗xe7 ♕xe7 11 ♗c4 ♘xc3 12 ♕xc3 c5 13 dxc5 ♕xc5 14 ♗b3 b6 15 ♕d2 ♕h5 16 ♗d1 ♘c5 17 b4 ♘e4 18 ♕d4 ♗b7 19 0-0 b5 20 ♘e5 ♕h6 21 ♘c6 ♗xc6 22 ♖xc6 ♘f6 23 ♗f3 ♖ad8 24 ♖d6 ♖xd6 25 ♕xd6 ♕h4 26 a3 ♕c4 27 ♕xa6 ♘d5 28 a4 ♘c7 29 ♕c6 ♕xc6 30 ♗xc6 bxa4 31 ♖a1 ♖b8 32 ♖xa4 ♔f8

Here's what Alekhine himself wrote:

"White's winning plan is easy to explain, but rather difficult to carry out. White exploits the fact that the black pieces are occupied on the queenside to create, by the gradual advance of his pawns and their exchange, vulnerable points in Black's position in the centre and on the kingside. Only after this preparatory work can the decisive offensive be begun."

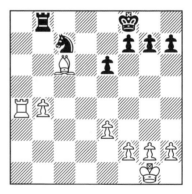

Note that Black's first 'weakness' is the pawn deficit on the queenside, whereas the second will be created on the kingside.

33 g4! ♔e7 34 b5 e5 35 f4 f6?!

Black wants to prevent White's rook from coming to d4 but this leaves him with a weak e5-pawn.

He could and should have played 35...exf4 when 36 exf4 gives White winning chances but nothing as clear as the game. Should White play 36 ♖d4, Black could save himself with 36...♘xb5 37 ♖b4 fxe3 38 ♗xb5 ♔d6 39 ♖b1 ♖b6 with a likely draw.

36 fxe5 fxe5 37 ♖a2

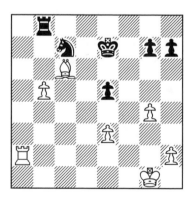

37...♖b6

White's last move prevented 37...♔d6 because of 38 ♖d2+ followed by 39 ♖d7.

38 ♖b2 h6 39 ♔f2 ♔e6 40 ♔f3 ♘d5

41 h4!

Declining the opportunity to go into a rook endgame and instead continuing to make progress on the kingside.

41...♘e7 42 ♗e4 ♘d5 43 ♖b3 ♔d6 44 g5! hxg5 45 hxg5

Now Black has a second weakness on g7 so the first stage is complete.

45...♔e6 46 ♗d3 ♔d6 47 ♖a3 ♘c7 48 ♖a7! ♖b8

48...♘xb5 49 ♖xg7 would be hopeless for Black.

49 ♔e4 g6

Otherwise White's king comes to f5.

50 ♖a3!

50...♖b6 51 ♗c4 ♖b8

After the alternative 51...♔c5 52 ♖a7 ♔xc4 (or 52...♘xb5 53 ♗xb5 ♔xb5 54 ♖e7) 53 ♖xc7+ ♔xb5 54 ♔xe5 Black would be losing the resultant rook endgame.

52 ♖d3+ ♔c5 53 ♖d7! ♘e8 54 ♗f7 ♘d6+ 55 ♔xe5 ♖b6 56 e4

56...♘xb5

Black has finally managed to eliminate the b-pawn but only at the cost of his entire kingside.

57 ♖d5+ ♔b4 58 ♖d8 ♘a7 59 ♖d6 ♘c6+ 60 ♔f6 ♔c5 61 ♖d5+ ♔b4 62 e5 ♔c4 63 ♖d1+ ♔c5 64 ♖c1+ ♔d4 65 e6 ♔e3 66 ♗xg6 ♘d4 67 ♗f7 ♘e2 68 ♖e1 1-0

50) Endgame understanding helps your middlegame

"In order to improve your game, you must study the endgame before everything else, for whereas the endings can be studied and mastered by themselves, the middle game and the opening must be studied in relation to the endgame."

José Raúl Capablanca

A common complaint by players I advise to study the endgame is that they rarely get one. But there are deeper reasons why someone should master this stage of the game.

First of all a player who has difficulty coordinating two or three pieces will clearly have difficulty with a board full of them; it makes perfect sense to study simple positions in order to understand more complex ones.

Secondly there is the issue that a fear of endgames can lead to players overdoing attempts to win in the middlegame and thereby overplaying their hand. The confidence to play endgames can lead to a more balanced approach to the middlegame whereby an exchange of pieces is allowed if it is the right thing to do.

In the following game Bobby Fischer shows his endgame confidence by allowing an early exchange of queens and then later swapping off his mighty knight on c5 for a very dodgy-looking black bishop.

Game 64
R.Fischer-T.Petrosian
Candidates Final (7th game),
Buenos Aires 1971
Sicilian Defence

---

1 e4 c5 2 ♘f3 e6 3 d4 cxd4 4 ♘xd4 a6 5 ♗d3 ♘c6 6 ♘xc6 bxc6 7 0-0 d5 8 c4!

Setting about attacking Black's d5-pawn and also introducing the possibility of the queen emerging with ♕d1-a4.

8 ♘d2 is a reasonable alternative for White but it is by no means as dangerous for Black.

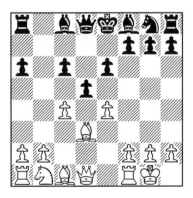

8...♘f6 9 cxd5 cxd5 10 exd5 exd5?

After this Black is clearly worse. Rather than accept an isolated pawn Black should probably have played

10...♕xd5!, with chances of equality.

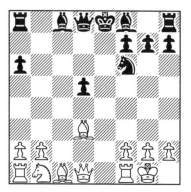

11 ♘c3! ♗e7 12 ♕a4+! ♕d7?!

Trying to bail out into an endgame whilst at the same time offering an exchange sacrifice by preparing to meet 13 ♗b5 with 13...axb5. But in view of White's powerful reply Black should probably have played just 12...♗d7 when 13 ♕c2! 0-0 14 ♗g5! d4 15 ♗xf6 ♗xf6 16 ♘e4 (16 ♗xh7+ ♔h8 threatens both the knight on c3 and 17...g6) 16...♗e7 is not too bad for Black.

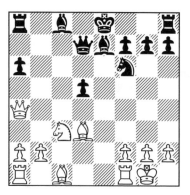

13 ♖e1!

Had Fischer not possessed such confidence in his endgame technique he might well have been tempted by 13

♗b5 axb5 14 ♕xa8, which is not at all clear after 14...0-0.

13...♕xa4 14 ♘xa4 ♗e6 15 ♗e3 0-0

After 15...♘d7 White can play 16 f4! g6 17 ♗d4 0-0 18 ♖ac1 with a clear advantage.

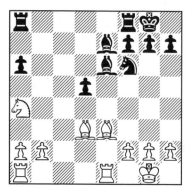

16 ♗c5!

For a second time Fischer refuses the lure of material, and rightly so. After 16 ♘b6 ♖ab8 17 ♗xa6 Black can play 17...d4 18 ♗xd4 ♖fd8 19 ♗e3 ♖d6, winning two pieces for a rook.

16...♖fe8 17 ♗xe7 ♖xe7

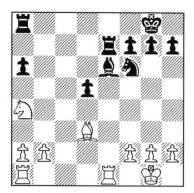

18 b4!

Fixing Black's weak a6-pawn whilst simultaneously strengthening the grip on the c5-square.

18...♚f8 19 ♘c5 ♝c8 20 f3 ♖ea7?!

After this passive move Black is probably lost. He should have challenged White's knight with 20...♘d7 after which 21 ♖ec1 is better for White but still a long way from a win.

21 ♖e5! ♝d7

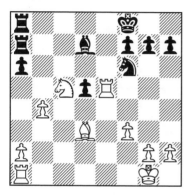

22 ♘xd7+!

A really remarkable move, typical of Fischer at his best. By exchanging off his powerful knight, White gains access to the c-file and is left with a strong bishop against a poor knight.

Polugaevsky suggested that 22 a4 would have been better, and this is the move that 95% of other Grandmasters would have played. But it is by no means as clear-cut.

22...♖xd7 23 ♖c1 ♖d6 24 ♖c7 ♘d7

After 24...♖e8 White has 25 ♖xe8+ ♚xe8 26 ♖a7.

25 ♖e2 g6 26 ♚f2 h5 27 f4 h4

The last chance to hang on was with 27...♘b6 28 ♖ee7 ♖f6.

28 ♚f3 f5 29 ♚e3 d4+

After 29...♘f6 White has 30 ♚d4 ♘e4 31 ♖ec2 with a winning position.

30 ♚d2 ♘b6 31 ♖ee7

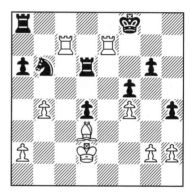

With not one but two rooks on the seventh rank, White dominates the position.

31...♘d5 32 ♖f7+ ♚e8 33 ♖b7 ♘xb4 34 ♝c4 1-0

There's no defence to the coming 35 ♖h7.

Index of Openings

Figures refer to page numbers.

Index of Games